# David Tutera

PHOTOGRAPHS BY
Charles and Jennifer Maring

## BULFINCH PRESS

NEW YORK · BOSTON

BULFINCH PRESS

Time Warner Book Group
1271 Avenue of the Americas, New York, NY 10020
Visit our Web site at www.bulfinchpress.com

First Edition

LIBRARY OF CONGRESS CATALOGING-IN-PUBLICATION DATA
Tutera, David.
The party planner / David Tutera ; photographs by Charles and Jennifer Maring.
    p. cm.
Includes index.
ISBN 0-8212-6165-7
1. Parties.  I. Title.
TX731.T87 2005         2004021614
793.2—dc22

Design by Vertigo Design NYC

PRINTED IN SINGAPORE

3 1558 00216 0422

Ryan . . . you are my angel.
YOU BRING ME STRENGTH, YOU BRING ME GUIDANCE,
AND YOU BRING ME A SENSE OF PEACE I NEVER KNEW BEFORE.
I LOVE YOU WITH ALL MY HEART AND SOUL.

# CONTENTS

# Introduction

You might think that after twenty years of planning parties I'd have it all figured out. I'd be like Batman: waiting for a sign in the night sky to tell me there's a party that needs me, then racing to the scene to instantly administer some trademark moves with reliable weapons of choice. I might sling a centerpiece that's always worked and suggest the trusty ecru place cards I always carry in my holster before vanishing. After that it's all just a matter of showing up to receive *another* tearful thank-you from the mayor for saving civilization. In actuality, my work is not like that (except for the last part, of course). I always strive to swoop in and save every event I design with the perfect idea, and on my TV show, *The Party Planner* (Discovery Channel), I often rescue "parties in distress." But there is just no secret weapon or formula for throwing the kind of passionate and imaginative parties that people never forget, and those are the parties I live and work for. So, if anything, a big part of what I've learned over the years is that, while a good superhero hones the same few superpowers, a good party planner never stops discovering new ones.

Frankly, I can't imagine working any other way, even though it would sure save time. I'm a busy guy — if I'm not choosing the flowers for the Official Post–Grammy Awards Party, I'm mapping a mountaintop wedding procession in snowy St. Moritz or lighting a backyard in Michigan for a romantic proposal dinner. But a formula would also spoil all the fun. I can't walk into a flea market without suddenly recognizing the *perfect* stone urn for a cocktail party I'm working on, let alone pass an upholstery shop without having a "tablecloth revelation" for a wedding in the works. I am endlessly inspired and constantly discovering new ideas, people, and places. Incidentally, one of the kernels of party-planning wisdom that I do rely on is this process of inspiration and discovery — it is crucial to a good party.

In fact, discovering the theme of a party means finding out about the person it's for. If I have honed anything like a superpower, it is the ability to render a particular client's abstract fantasy of an event in actual details that he or she can experience in reality. In the parties that fill this book, I translate romantic memories of Tuscany's rolling hills into a three-dimensional table runner built from undulating waves of wine-colored roses. I channel the childlike anticipation at the sight of unopened

Christmas presents through whimsically sophisticated light fixtures wrapped up like gifts. Sometimes this process builds on a space. For instance, the sight of a client's bountiful herb garden inspired me to trade the usual centerpiece of cut flowers for a dramatic display of fresh herbs and orange zinnia, all planted together in stone urns, for her outdoor anniversary dinner. Other times, this process totally transforms an area. I'll never forget the night I made over a Boston garage as a Chinatown street party complete with colorful paper dragon kites, the scent of five different spices in the air, and sparklers in hand. In short, I blend the details of people's memories, visions, and personalities with the spirit of the celebration at hand to produce a vivid and lively reality.

Maybe all this talk of magic and transformation — or the very idea of the "Tutera touch" — *sounds* like the stuff of X-ray goggles and Batmobiles, but Superman can't teach you how to fly. I, on the other hand, have put together the detailed party descriptions in this book to help those who love to entertain as much as I do incorporate some of the lessons I've learned in *my* process of discovery into their *own* processes. If it is any one thing, the "Tutera touch" is the one tangible detail in a sea of decorations that just glows with the energy and joy that plucked it from the realm of individual fantasy to make it real; it's the wow-factor that you can only imagine one party at a time. That's why I've broken every party into five sections, each of which focuses on one of the five senses. Fantasies are made real only through practical, human sensations. You don't just find yourself experiencing the sun-kissed, laid-back wonder of a teenager at the Jersey Shore when you're christening a new boat in a pair of (decidedly adult) linen pants; you see the broad, multicolored stripes of beach towels past, you smell the "boardwalk fries" and salt on the wind, and you feel the texture of canvas and the warmth of hurricane lamps. It is this attention to sensation that makes a party mean something totally unique to the people who share it, and whether this book provides you with literal blueprints or fleeting inspirations, it is designed to help you create such parties.

At the same time, this book functions as an essential primer for planning different kinds of events. Each party fits into one of four larger sections on cocktail parties, holiday entertaining, dinner parties, or milestone celebrations. I'll help you master the subtle theatrical art of keeping spirits high when drinks are in order, coax the inner child out of any holiday event with decidedly sophisticated flair, turn the feel of a sit-down dinner into one of riveting enchantment, and show every single guest at a loved one's special occasion how to take part in its significance. Every step of the way I'll describe creative ways to add a touch of mystery and surprise — two of my favorite ways to play with the senses — to every imaginable type of party. And, maybe by the end, when the image of a certain place setting lingers in your mind's eye, or the weave of a particular tablecloth seems to dance on your fingertips, you'll agree that designing a party with a personal touch isn't the stuff of superpowers or magic; it just *feels* that way.

# 1

## COCKTAIL PARTIES

FIRE AND ICE: A WINTER BLUES PARTY

SUMMER NIGHTS: A SHIP-TO-SHORE PARTY

Entertaining is a lot like theater: You set the stage of your life for a special night and share its meaning with others. Like most plays, there's usually some organizing focal point or narrative that commands the attention of everyone, whether it's a ritual, a meal, or a "starring" guest. But the cocktail party is different. It is the interactive theater of entertaining, the sum of energy and motion and people. At cocktail parties, the action and the stars aren't confined to one moment or one space; the story is open because it *is* the crowd.

But even the craziest kinds of theater need directors, and the same is true of a good cocktail party. I've been to some with no direction, where people meet, mingle, and network, and leave after thirty minutes when they run out of business cards. Yuck. But who can blame them? Yes, a cocktail party can kill lots of birds with one efficient martini, from mixing different faces and making connections, to kicking off a larger event, or quickly catching up with chums old and new. But if there's no dramatic tension in the room, no sense of movement, what should feel like a party ends up feeling more like a product launch or an infomercial; you tune out once you see the Flowbee do its magic. Don't let this happen to you. You

want your cocktail party to feel like *the* place to be, and in order to keep it that way, you as the host, will have to give it a plot.

Everyone knows that you can't create a sense of excitement without a little advance buzz, but not everyone knows how effectively a well-designed invitation can do this. Mailing out a fabulous invitation that hints at the color scheme, tone, and formality of the party is the equivalent of a glowing advance review. But don't forget: People can't buzz about intangibles. You must also account for all of the nitty-gritty details, which includes mentioning the word "cocktails," the RSVP info, the attire, and the full time period of the party, but not obvious things, like the presence of snacks. People want to be in scenes they've already imagined, and if your guests dress the part and plan their time accordingly, they will begin the evening with that crucial spark that plugs them into an anticipated event.

OFFER YOUR GUESTS A PROGRESSIVE SELECTION OF TASTES.

Of course, once they arrive, almost everything else boils down to the creation of a lively space, where people feel fabulous and dynamic both physically and mentally. My favorite way to do this is to choreograph the movement of guests around a careful arrangement of food, drinks, decorations, and each other. And, hey, because we're talking about a cocktail party, this whole science begins with the bar: Always put it as far from the front door as possible. Once you've greeted guests at the door with the offer of a beverage — you should *always* be the first person they see — they'll feel totally welcome, and ready to move deeper into the fray, if only to wet their whistles. Already, you will have set possible interactions into motion . . . consider this Act One.

The next challenge will be to keep things fresh. Cocktail parties should feel a little like a volleyball game without the kneepads or grunts — every so often you *rotate!* If you set up displays of simple snacks like olives, hors d'oeuvres, and such in interesting places all over the entertaining space, people will be drawn to the far corners. I'll say it again: Do not, I repeat, do not situate all the food in one big feeding zone. Create different stations for different flavors, taking advantage of coffee tables, kitchen islands, sideboards, and the like, and half the dance has already been syncopated. Also, guests who spread out in clusters will not only have more intimate conversations, they'll have an excuse to get out of them when they're ready to hunt down the canapé they saw go by from another part of the room.

Of course, this clever arrangement doesn't take care of the question of suspense, but I have one other food presentation technique that does: Offer your guests a progressive selection of tastes. If you begin by setting out simple morsels like cheese, nuts, and crudités, then introduce a few new items in the second hour of the party, and so on — perhaps something that plays a *slightly* more substantial role, but we're not talking Brando material. Your guests will feel a sense of development and, voilà, your narrative is in motion. Another great thing about this technique is that it allows your guests to nibble consistently throughout the night without tiring of the same old thing, an amenity that may be the difference between a bright, wonderful feeling of levity and a terrible feeling of wooziness. So this rule is an essential one: Never serve martinis or other potent drinks without food. The elegance they affect so well is lost once the room is moving around people instead of the other way around.

Once you've mapped out the flow of the room through the placement of food and drink, you'll be ready to tackle the decorations, another essential element of cocktail vibe. On the most basic level, the principles are the same. Don't put all your flowers in one basket: Spread decorations evenly throughout the space so people don't perceive any central place to be. Instead of fretting over one centerpiece, scatter vases with fresh flowers or elements of the design motif throughout all active rooms. Don't forget to be practical about the positioning of small tables, where guests can perch their drinks and pick up napkins, and the placement of discreet trash receptacles, where they can unload olive pits and other refuse. Walking through a room and seeing surfaces covered with half-eaten food and wadded up napkins is not sexy, and a cocktail party should always be a little sexy. The only other fundamental rule of decoration is dim lighting. On the off-chance that your guests have come straight from work, it will either make them feel more glammed up or make them less self-conscious.

Any way you slice it, low lights create a distinctly loose feel to a room, and will only further encourage motion and mystery.

I confess: There is only so much you can do to a space to make it dynamic. After a certain point, you have to create movement the old-fashioned way, with your own two feet. No cocktail party is complete without *some* kind of music, although it should never overwhelm the volume of the conversation in the room. And because music always tends to make people move, it helps a lot with establishing a certain energy level. In fact, a live jazz band or singer only increases these good vibrations, but if you hire one, make sure to let forty-five minutes or so pass before they start; this delay will allow your guests to settle in and establish their celebratory momentum.

Finally, and perhaps most importantly, is your own movement as host. If you don't mingle and enjoy yourself, then how can your guests? I always advise my clients to plan out some basic introductions between people they think might get along. This way, without getting caught up in a long conversation (unless you want to!), you can simply forge a connection and move about the room. Another great trick for greasing the cocktail party wheels is enlisting a partner. Every one has at least one gregarious friend who just radiates warmth; put him or her to use. This strategy will be particularly helpful in the last half hour of the party, when you should finally break all the previous rules and station yourself at the door to say good-byes, arrange car services, defuse any parking crises, or help with coats. Just as you should always be the *first* person your guests see upon entering the party, you should always be the *last*. After all, at the end of a rousing theater production, when the elaborate orchestration has gone off without a hitch, the audience always loves to see a great director step forward to take a final bow. But you can do even better. In the following chapter, I'll take you through every step you need to know to throw a legendary cocktail party. We'll hit the shores for a boat christening in the style of an old-school boardwalk bash and we'll heat up a shivering night with a "Fire and Ice" cocktail party, sure to melt the winter blues away. Using these tips, strategies, designs, and ideas, I guarantee one heck of a curtain call.

Depending on what kind of space you have

TO WORK WITH, IT CAN BE CHALLENGING TO ACTUALLY

CREATE A COCKTAIL PARTY THAT INSPIRES THAT OH-SO-

ESSENTIAL ELEMENT OF DYNAMIC MOVEMENT AND MOOD.

IN FACT, SOMETIMES IT FEELS MORE LIKE A PHYSICS PROBLEM

THAN A PARTY CONCEPT. WHAT IF YOU HAVE ONLY ONE ROOM

TO WORK WITH? WHAT IF IT'S ON THE "COZY" SIDE?

HOW MANY CLOWNS CAN FIT INTO A VOLKSWAGEN

AND STILL MANAGE TO HAVE A GOOD TIME?

ON THE FRIGID JANUARY DAY when I first met Zach and Kimberly Barocas at the venue they hoped to use for a cocktail party, these and other great questions of the universe ran through my head.

I often advise my clients to rent out private rooms from restaurants because they offer an economical alternative to jazzing up the homestead, with certain party essentials (like furniture and a commercial kitchen) already in place. Amuse, the lovely little restaurant in New York City's Chelsea district, where this particular party would be held, is one of those gems in the New York restaurant scene that radiates charm. But Zach and Kimberly wanted to reward twenty-two colleagues and clients with a lively, imaginative evening of fun after winning a big account for their small business, and charm alone just doesn't guarantee letting one's hair down. In order to create the sleek, modern affair that these two young entrepreneurs had in mind and make it feel loose and energetic for the number of guests invited, I realized I would need to bust out the smoke and mirrors.

And that's when it hit me: Surfaces of mirrors and Lucite would make the perfect marriage of form and function for this late winter celebration.

They create the illusion of even more action and energy — you literally see more people throughout the room — but at the same time, the combination of clear and reflective materials instantly makes the room feel more open. Even more importantly, they capture the striking beauty of a late blast of winter weather in clean, contemporary lines. Every winter, while driving between New York and Connecticut, I marvel at the ice formations covering the rocky bluffs along the highway. On a clear day, when the promise of spring fills the air with light and heat, the gleaming sun brings out the deepest, most sparkling, beautiful blues from those frozen depths. It's that sensation of fire and ice, hot and cold, that washes away my winter blues, and it's that same sensation that I wanted to create at Zach and Kimberly's celebration, which fell on a chilly March night. So, along with the ice-like surfaces and funky blue fabrics that would bring out the swing in this modernist vision of winter, spicy, flavorful tapas, and hot Latin rhythms would raise the pulse and temperature of the room. It would be like a prize-fight between January and July! And if the high energy and warm spirit of this chic cocktail party were any indication, the mercury would catch up to the music soon enough.

# The Look

## CHILLY ON THE OUTSIDE, CHILI PEPPERS ON THE INSIDE

Capturing the smooth, glassy surfaces of icicles, and the shimmering icy blue hues of freshly fallen snow can be tricky; you don't want to go overboard and end up with a truly "cold," severe look. Instead, you want to create a magical cavern of shimmering shapes and reflective surfaces that will make your guests feel as though they are surrounded by gorgeous Steuben crystal sculptures. There are plenty of ways to achieve the twinkle of crystal without using too much of the real thing. For Zach and Kimberly, I crafted a custom Lucite table with a boxlike tabletop and then filled that with a flurry of white and two shades of (dyed) blue carnation petals. Atop the table, I created small pyramids of Lucite boxes for the tapas display. Around this, I placed Lucite Philippe Starck Louis Ghost Chairs — a nod to the modern-design concept for the room, as well as a convenient pit stop for guests preferring to sit while snacking on the buffet of delicious foods.

A series of small cocktail tables were draped in ice-blue dupioni silk tablecloths and an outrageous metallic blue shag fabric was added to the borders. Further from the table, in the "lounging" area, I placed ottomans and lampshades (also covered in metallic blue shag) in cozy corners. As the finishing touches were completed, I started to get really excited but it was when the large mirrors arrived that my dream of a shimmering, expansive space really took off. Mirrors have been used to "enlarge" rooms since the beginning of time; they work beautifully on walls, leaning against them or hanging at an angle from the ceiling ("brasserie style"). For a special party atmosphere they not only double your space, they also double your decor!

And speaking of decor, I want to backtrack and offer a quick word on the subject of carnations. Do not look down your nose on these affordable blossoms. They're just a few dollars a dozen, and seem to be in every supermarket on Valentine's Day, but they are, in essence, a lovely flower. Perhaps this is why they caught on in the first place. I've used bouquets of bold, colorful carnations as quick pick-me-ups for a simple Easter lunch, or peppered fluffy pale pink ones into larger floral arrangements to add a little softness and poof to the design. Most of all, what I love about carnations is that you can buy them inexpensively in bulk quantities to use for creative displays, such as the mosaic I dreamed up here.

# A "Winter Blues" Carnation Petal Mosaic

- Choose a color scheme and purchase carnations in those colors.

- Cut the petals off fresh carnations, keeping as much of the petal intact as possible.

- Be sure to separate the colors.

- Neatly pile the petals in a square-tiled pattern (as I did on the coffee table) or create your own pattern. Let your imagination go wild!

### COCO-FABULOUS

Just shy of cracking open a new bottle of Hawaiian Tropic Dark Tanning Oil, I went all out to create the aromatic atmosphere of an island retreat for this ice-blue affair. Mind you, sometimes packaged "tropical scents" can really tweak the nostrils a little too hard. Imagine a banana-scented (and shaped) car air-freshener hanging from a rearview mirror and you'll know just what I mean. Instead, I used all natural ingredients to achieve a truly coco-fabulous scent.

Starting with a few gardenias in the usual spots — by the front door, in the powder room, and by the coat check — I added some floral perfumes where the carnations (as much as I love them) could provide none. Then I let the roasting pistachios, simmering coconut broth, and sizzling chorizo send their wonderful tangy and nutty aromas into the party space. Finally, guests got a fresh and fruity pick-me-up just from standing near the bar, where pineapple and passion fruit juices were flowing freely into the night.

# The Touch

## SMOOTH AS ICE

The surface of ice is so beautiful to behold — imagine the pristine gloss of newly frozen lake or the sex appeal of a few shapely ice cubes jostling in a glass tumbler. The touch of ice, however, is not always so nice — imagine the thud of a ski-spill on "black ice" or the burning sensation of holding a packet of frozen vegetables too long. To wipe away the winter blues for Zack and Kimberly's guests, I decided to couple all of the imagery of glassy ice surfaces without the freeze of subzero temperatures. Take, for example, the plastic "ice-cube" lights I piled inside the Lucite boxes and placed in each cocktail glass to add a mod, almost sci-fi blue glow to the room and the drinks. Guests enjoyed a warm smoothness all around them: They could sit on Lucite chairs, admire themselves in mirrors, and eat from blue glass plates with shimmering silverware. Smooth surfaces like these worked to create an ice-palace feeling, but they can also be applied to most contemporary parties. I use Lucite boxes in the summer for holding sand, shells, and water to create miniature seascapes, and in the spring as pools for floating orchids or gerbera daisies. Either way, I always notice guests running their hands along the clear and even surfaces.

# The Taste

One of the best ways to add a little bit of mystery and drama to a cocktail party is to mix up the menu with lots of bold flavors and bright accents. That's why I imported a quintessential tradition of Spanish dining for Zach and Kimberly's upbeat shindig: tapas-style (small) plates. Tapas — taken from the word *tapar*, meaning "to cover" — were originally offered as a simple little bite included in the price of a sherry or a beer at the local bar, bodega, or tascas. Proprietors quickly realized that if they offered a salty slice of cured ham or a few olives on the tiny dish that protected the cocktails they served from those pesky fruit flies, customers lingered to enjoy the conversations and the drinks just a little longer. But since then, tapas have not only grown in popularity, they have grown in complexity.

Although you can still charm guests with a simple plate of cured meats and cheeses or a few nuts, you can also serve more substantial dishes that appease larger and more elaborate appetites, from marinated fish to braised, seasoned vegetables. The point is to sample a variety of flavors on a smaller scale and feed a sense of sociability in the process. At a winter cocktail party, where the emphasis on food should always be a little greater to quiet that hibernating impulse, tapas-style dishes offer an intriguing array of exciting, sustaining tastes.

Because so much of this party's fiery side would come from the menu, Gerry Hayden (Executive Chef of Amuse Restaurant) and I selected a

## Winter Blues Cocktail Tapas Menu

Courtesy of Amuse Restaurant, New York City, Gerry Hayden, Executive Chef and Managing Partner

ASSORTED BABY BEETS, GOAT CHEESE, AND ROASTED PISTACHIOS OVER A BED OF BABY GREENS

YELLOWFIN TUNA SASHIMI AND SOBA NOODLES WITH CHINESE PARSLEY ESSENCE AND SPICY SOY LIME DRESSING

BUTTER POACHED LOBSTER WITH COCONUT BROTH AND CLAMSHELL MUSHROOMS

GRILLED CHORIZO AND FINGERLING POTATOES WITH GREEN ONIONS AND SHERRY VINEGAR

DUCK PROSCIUTTO AND MELON SALAD WITH UPLAND CRESS AND SPICED PISTACHIOS

series of dishes that would tantalize guests with exciting combinations of sweet and smoky spices. And, of course, we added that crucial sense of suspense to the evening by offering a few new food flavors every hour or so. Upon arrival, for instance, guests nibbled on the basics: nuts, cheese, and salami. Gradually, new, more complex flavors roused the senses: a salad of beets, goat cheese, and roasted pistachios over baby greens appetized guests with a perfect balance of creamy and crunchy textures; the purest, most precise cut of tuna sashimi became a Japanese twist on ceviche with a piquant citrus dressing and a bracing puree of Chinese parsley. Perhaps most enticing of all, the soft, mellow sweetness of lobster poached in coconut broth made guests swoon to the samba, while the smoky tones of red-hot chorizo and rich duck prosciutto paired with brighter, more acidic counterpoints formed a deep, searing baseline in this high-energy dance of flavors. *Caliente,* indeed.

## DRAGON TAIL

1 ounce Belvedere Cytrus Vodka

1 ounce lychee juice

1 ounce pineapple juice

Pineapple wedge and lychee nut for garnish

Shake, strain, and pour into martini glass. Garnish with pineapple wedge and lychee nut on kebob.

## MIDNIGHT MARTINI

1 ounce Belvedere Pomarańcza Vodka

¾ ounce Blue Curaçao

½ ounce passion fruit juice

½ ounce pineapple juice

Orange slice for garnish

Shake, strain, and pour into martini glass. Garnish with orange slice.

## PARADISIMO

1 ounce ruby red or pink grapefruit juice

1 ounce gin

Red grapefruit for garnish

Shake, strain, and pour into martini glass. Garnish with red grapefruit flesh (no skin).

## WINTER BLUE MARTINI

1 ounce Belvedere Pomarańcza  Vodka

½ ounce Blue Curaçao

½ ounce crème de cassis

Splash of fresh lime juice

Blueberries for garnish

Rim martini glass with white sugar. Shake, strain, and pour liquid ingredients into martini glass. Garnish with blueberry kebob.

# The Sound

Nothing heats up a room quite like a Latin beat. In fact, whenever I'm rushing down the sidewalks of New York in the dead of winter, I build up a little rumba beat in my head and I instantly feel warmer. I don't exactly peel off layers, but I definitely feel closer to the equator. Needless to say, Zach and Kimberly's guests chased away the winter blues to the beats of tango, merengue, flamenco, and salsa. As we changed the tempos every half hour and added spurts of current pop songs to keep folks on their toes, the music rose and fell, but the intoxicating energy level did not.

A little samba will set guests at ease as they settle into a new atmosphere and say their hellos. Rosa Passos's *Azul* is an especially great choice for this stage of the evening, but most compilations of samba bossa nova will also light a perfectly pale fire. Here are more music options to get your guests dancing:

*Buena Vista Social Club* soundtrack

Bette Midler: *For the Boys,* "Baby, It's Cold Outside"

Judy Garland: *The Best of Judy Garland in Hollywood,* "Get Happy"

The Pointer Sisters: *The Very Best of the Pointer Sisters: Fire,* "Fire"

Pat Benatar: *Best Shots,* "Fire and Ice"

Jamiroquai: *Funk Odyssey*

*Buddah-Bar,* all six volumes

*The Best of Cafe Del Mar*

Gipsy Kings: *The Best of the Gipsy Kings*

Once you're really ready to shake things up, break out the serious salsa. Stan Kenton's *Cuban Fire!* will light a flame under, well, pretty much anything. I also love Sonora Carruseles's *Heavy Salsa* and more eclectic mixes,

like the incomparable and innovative *Latin Groove* (from the Putumayo music label). But, whatever you do, don't forget the late, great Celia Cruz, or you will hear about it from true fans of salsa. Besides, her final Cuban-influenced collection of salsa, *Regalo del Alma,* is beyond compare.

Isn't it funny how one little simple detail or one brief moment can totally transform the feeling of a party? When Zach and Kimberly's guests first arrived, fully decked out in their best business casual, I have to admit I was a little uncertain about whether or not they'd be able to leave the office behind for the other worldly landscape I'd constructed. In the first half hour, they gingerly sipped their drinks and wore the pained expressions of people who were secretly dreaming of removing their respective high heels and ties. But a change of pace occurred when the second wave of music filled the air with the irresistible rhythms of salsa! Let me just say that rugs were cut. The volume of laughter and conversation rose with the melody as people shuffled between the lounge area and the more intimate cocktail table settings as they explored the room. Faces lit up as every new dish added fragrant new spices to the air. As those ties loosened up and the heels came off, it was as if the whole room finally fell into step, playing it cool while also heating things up. And, sure enough, before the end of the night, the snow stopped.

# Tutera Tips

1  Display bottles of vodka frozen inside decorative ice blocks: Cut off the top section of an orange juice container and fill it two thirds full with distilled water and sliced lemons, limes, and oranges. Insert a bottle of Belvedere Cytrus vodka and put in the freezer overnight. In the morning, remove the orange juice carton and you've got yourself a stunning citrus ice sculpture that doubles as a "cooler" for your vodka.

2  To give a martini an extra "kick," rub the rim of the glass with a slice of a hot jalapeño pepper. Dip the glass in sugar, and voilà! This is the perfect garnish for a sweet and fiery martini.

3  When cleaning Lucite, use a mild soap-and-water solution or a specialty cleanser. Never use your household window cleaner as it can cause the Lucite to dull and fog.

4  Always remember to create levels when serving a meal buffet style and, at the same time, make sure the food is easily accessible.

5  For a colorful cocktail, try using store-bought blue "ice cube" lights. These fake ice cubes come in a variety of fun colors. You can also make colorful ice cubes by adding food coloring or sliced fruits to your ice trays before freezing.

6  For a fun and easy cocktail centerpiece, place colored ice in a pretty glass bowl (about three quarters full) and decorate with a gardenia on top. Not only will this potent flower add a wonderful fragrance to the room, but once the ice melts you will have a floating gardenia.

7  To avoid watering down a pitcher of premixed cocktails, add a ziplock bag filled with ice to the pitcher. This will help keep the cocktail chilled without diluting the drinks!

8  Send your invitations in a miniature cobalt blue Lucite box to set a cool, disco-like ice-palace tone for the night.

9  If a custom Lucite tabletop is not at your disposal, consider a runner comprised of multiple Lucite boxes, each filled with weightless piles of carnation petals. Alternating petal colors make a striking statement. This look works any time of year — just be cautious of using loose petals in the burning sunshine of a hot summer day.

10  Create a mosaic of flower petals on any table (whether on a series of plates, or directly on a glass tabletop) by arranging different colored petals in bold geometric patterns.

## SUMMER NIGHTS:
## A SHIP-TO-SHORE PARTY
*for twenty-five*

For Steven and Alexa, who grew up

VACATIONING AT THE JERSEY SHORE, NO SUMMER COULD

EVER BE COMPLETE WITHOUT A LARGE SERVING OF BOARDWALK

FRIES AND A COUPLE OF LIME FREEZE POPS. WHEN THEY FIRST

ASKED ME TO HELP PLAN A SUMMER COCKTAIL PARTY FOR THE

OCCASION OF THEIR BOAT CHRISTENING, I HAD AN IDEA THEY

WERE THINKING MORE ALONG THE LINES OF SNOW CONES AND

FLIP-FLOPS THAN MOËT & CHANDON AND MANOLO MULES.

ALTHOUGH THEIR BEACH HOUSE ON LONG ISLAND is miles from the nearest rickety roller coaster or whirring cotton-candy machine, these two were determined to make their boat christening a fun, breezy reminder of all those wonderful, windswept nights of their Jersey Shore youth. All I had to hear were the words "saltwater taffy" and I knew where we were headed. My mind flooded with images of the shore. The trick, I soon realized, was to update images of sunburned teenagers devouring fried food between gulps of Dr. Pepper to images of sensibly bronzed adults nibbling on bite-sized burgers while never losing that feeling of youthful summertime bliss. That back-in-the-day, beachy feeling would need just a little refining.

I ALWAYS DESCRIBE GREAT ENTERTAINING AS TRANSPORTING GUESTS TO ANOTHER WORLD.

In order to update Steven and Alexa's teenage board-walk fantasy to a sophisticated grown-up reality, I turned to a few of my favorite seaside motifs: stripes, seashells, and simple bright colors. This kind of cheerful and clean decor would add a nice structure to the expanse of washboard pier and gray-blue ocean before us. We could lose the sandy flip-flops and sticky Coppertone sheen, but there was no way I was going to forgo the boardwalk fries, burgers, colorful drinks, bonfire s'mores, and amusement-park sweets. All that was required was a little updating of presentation. (And really good fries!) In place of the flickering lights of the boardwalk, I opted for hurricane candles that lined the pier and glittered throughout the party, and in place of Dr. Pepper I created a colorful menu of cocktails. Even the feeling of lounging *under* the boardwalk was suggested by a large spread of soft, striped beach towels. Guests could kick off their shoes and stare up at the stars while finishing off an old-fashioned ice-cream sandwich.

We also wanted to play up the boat christening without insisting that guests rock the *whole* night away on deck. Don't get me wrong, Steven and Alexa have a divine boat, well worthy of a christening, but it was no *Pacific Princess* and the reality of feeding and entertaining twenty nicely dressed adults on board was a concern. Looking back, I am truly grateful that this problem presented itself. The solution added more momentum to the party than any fruity cocktail or Top 40 hit could. After a little head scratching and pacing, it came to me: We would gather guests at one location and then deliver them to the "party dock" on board the new boat. When the boat approached, the illuminated cocktail-party area and streams of bright ribbon could be seen flowing from canvas umbrellas, and excitement amongst the guests mounted. Upon docking, each guest was greeted by a "red carpet" of striped canvas which led to a table of colorful cocktails. I always describe great entertaining as transporting guests to another world, so you can imagine how much I loved literally transporting Steven and Alexa's friends to a magical location. The success of this party "launch" made me consider: Who needs the *Pacific Princess* when you've got *Fantasy Island* waiting for you?

# The Look

When we think of the beach, we imagine golden sunshine, blue skies and water, and white sand. In short, we see bright colors. It's hard to think of the ocean without sunlight, but it's important that you do so when planning a seaside cocktail party; once the sun goes down it can get very dark out there. The sea takes on a deep moody hue and the sand seems only a wavy, shadowy carpet beneath the starry sky. What does this mean to a party planner? When you're entertaining by the sea and at night, lighting is everything. And, to make matters more complicated, you've got a lot of untamable wind to contend with. If you don't plan (and test) your lighting, you might find yourself dashing around with a lighter all night, trying to relight candles. My recommendation is to tackle the lighting first so you're off to a good start.

For Steven and Alexa's dock party, I lined the pier with pillar candles stabilized in galvanized buckets. I used large and small glass hurricanes to protect dozens and dozens of candles and placed them along the edges of the dock, around the tables, along the pier, and bordering the surrounding lawn. To add extra support for the candles and to add color, I poured alternating layers of bright yellow and blue sand into each hurricane and wedged the candles into this striped sand base. To illuminate the buffet table (and to echo the shape of the paper boardwalk French-fry containers), I lodged cone-shaped glass votive holders into sand-filled galvanized buckets. Finally, at the end of the party, sparklers were distributed for an invigorating miniature light show.

The party "lighting," however, didn't end with the actual lights, but extended to the color palette. In an effort to boost the stone-colored pier into action and keep a bright boardwalk feeling alive, I decorated the party with bursts of sunflower yellow, boating blue, primary red, and hints of sailcloth whites and canvas beige. Each guest received a bright red-and-white invitation enclosed in a red cardboard box along with a miniature

wood boat and a note reading, "We're going overboard." These cute invites set the neo-preppy, colorful tone for the party. Then I went to town with a yellow-, blue-, and red-striped motif. The tables were trimmed with striped canvas, the lawn blanketed with striped beach towels, the fries wrapped in striped paper cones, the galvanized buckets tied with striped ribbon, and even the colorful cocktails were arranged in a striped pattern on the cocktail table. I added seashells to the tables in small clusters and sewed small white sand dollars to the edges of each tablecloth. For a final touch, I attached yellow and blue ribbons to the canvas umbrellas. They fluttered and danced in the breeze as if the stripes had suddenly come to life. As the sun lowered over Long Island Sound, the brilliant colors and dazzling candlelight kept the mood lively. It also prevented guests from taking an unplanned stroll off the pier, which would surely take the party's theme of "we're going overboard" one step too far.

# HOW TO MAKE
## A Beach Towel Blanket

- Cut old beach towels into equal-sized squares, approximately 2 square feet.

- Sew the squares together, so that no like colors / patterns are touching — make as large or small as you like.

- Sew a ribbon or edging around the entire border of the blanket to keep from fraying.

- Put a grommet in each of the four corners. Thread a thin rope through each grommet.

- Use four stakes to hold down each of the four corners — perfect for a picnic or the beach!

# The Scent

FROM SEA SALT . . . TO SALTY FRIES

If you've ever taken an evening stroll down a busy boardwalk and been able to resist the lure of hot, salty French fries, sugar-coated fried dough, double-scoop ice-cream cones, or a real American burger, I am forced to wonder if you have any sense of smell at all. Get me within a few blocks of the bustle of any boardwalk worth its weight in cotton candy and my mouth is watering. Maybe it has something to do with the hunger earned from a day of frolicking in the waves, but mostly I think it's the drifting, seductive aroma of the almighty French fry that does me in. In "Under the Boardwalk," the Drifters crooned, *"You can almost taste the hot dogs / And French fries they sell . . ."* These are exactly the kind of appetite triggers I wanted to pull for Steven and Alexa's unsuspecting guests, and how easy it was to achieve! I simply made sure that at least some of the food preparation was within range of the party. I set up a small barbecue for the miniburgers and s'mores in the mingling area. Not far off, the French fries sizzled. The sea breezes, themselves a little salty, carried these aromas around the party like a tray of hors d'oeuvres, tempting folks to indulge in another delicious trip back to the buffet table.

## WIND IN THE SAILS

I'm all for the feeling of sand between my toes, but when it comes right down to it, I think I prefer the feeling of *washing away* the sand and drying off with a nice, big beach towel. So, with this sensation in mind — the *clean* beach feeling — I focused on assembling a series of windswept, smooth surfaces for this seaside cocktail affair. I hung cocktail napkins from a clothesline with bleached wooden pegs. The colorful cloths danced back and forth in the breeze like miniature sails flapping against the wind. I spread a patchwork of towels over the grass so that guests could luxuriate in the feeling of thick terrycloth against their skin. I opted for soft canvas deck chairs, tablecloths, and umbrellas. To contrast these gentle surfaces, I added some good old rugged boating textures to the mix: roping around glass hurricanes, bark, and coral; rough seashells glued on candleholders in decorative clusters; wind-worn shutters for serving trays and tabletops; and two old sawhorses for the buffet table base. Even the food reflected these soft-over-rough surfaces, most especially when we set about melting chocolate over crunchy graham crackers and squeezable marshmallows!

## SALTY, SWEET, AND GRILLED OVER THE FIRE

Alexa and I worked on the menu together. Right from the get-go we referred to it as our "Back-in-the-Day Menu." We stayed true to our boardwalk-loving roots and selected miniature hamburgers, small grilled sandwiches, and paper cones of salty boardwalk fries. I added a touch of sophistication with three different dipping sauces for the fries: honey mustard, spicy ranch, and BBQ. We also chose miniature lobster rolls, vodka-marinated cherry tomatoes, and fresh oysters on the shell. All of these savory treats were served as individual portions from a continually replenished buffet bar. I created two eating areas: a picnic spot (decorated with spread towels, picnic baskets, and small tables made from upturned galvanized buckets and old shutters) and a cocktail-seating area on the dock. The desserts were as retro as the appetizers: trays of freeze pops, ice-cream sandwiches, saltwater taffy, old-fashioned candy, frozen chocolates, brownies, s'mores, and skewers of fresh fruit topped with lychee juice. In total, we provided a real all-American dinner, just in bite-sized cocktail-party portions. Looking back, I remember that we originally assumed guests would choose how to spend their appetites. Now that the party has come and gone, though, I can assure you that while some folks picked burgers over oysters, or oysters over lobster rolls, there was not one guest who passed on the boardwalk fries.

## RED SIZZLE

2 ounces Belvedere Cytrus Vodka

½ ounce apricot brandy

½ ounce fresh lemon juice

½ ounce passion fruit liqueur

Swedish Fish for garnish

Pour into cocktail shaker with ice. Shake, strain, and pour into a martini glass. Garnish with a Swedish Fish.

## BLUE WAVE

2 ounces gin

1 ounce Blue Curaçao

Splash of Cointreau

Club soda

Key lime for garnish

Pour gin, Blue Curaçao, and Cointreau in a highball glass with ice. Fill with club soda and stir. Garnish with a key lime slice.

## SUMMER SPARKLER

2 ounces Belvedere Pomarańcza Vodka

4 dashes bitters

½ ounce fresh lemon juice

Splash of Moët & Chandon champagne

Red sugar for rim

Peach slice for garnish

Pour first three ingredients into a cocktail shaker with ice. Shake, strain, and pour into a martini glass rimmed in red sugar. Top with a splash of champagne. Garnish with a peach slice.

# The Sound

"UNDER THE BOARDWALK . . ."

The sound of the ocean lapping up against the wooden pier does it for me every time. It is all I need to feel like a real California dreamer. I could sit and listen to the water for hours. Having said that, the sound of rolling waves and the odd foghorn may be great for contemplating the stars up above, but I was planning a real swinging boardwalk-style cocktail party for a boat christening! Since this wasn't a back-to-nature retreat, we needed some good summer cocktail-party music. A rule of thumb: ALWAYS have some dance music at a cocktail party. Whether you expect guests to break out onto the floor or not, upbeat music is important — with just enough rhythm to get the hips swaying at the cocktail bar. The energy level is what to focus on. Here's a sampling of music for this kind of gathering:

Pottery Barn's *Summer Vibes*

Bette Midler: *Bette Midler Sings the Rosemary Clooney Songbook,* with my favorite, "On a Slow Boat to China"

Bobby Darin: *As Long as I'm Singing: The Bobby Darin Collection,* "Beyond the Sea"

Sheryl Crow: *C'mon C'mon,* "Soak Up the Sun"

Jimmy Buffett: *Meet Me in Margaritaville: The Ultimate Collection,* "Margaritaville"

Bob Marley: *Legend: The Best of Bob Marley and the Wailers*

The Beach Boys: *Sounds of Summer*

The Mamas & the Papas: *Greatest Hits,* with everyone's favorite summertime song, "California Dreaming"

Martha & the Vandellas: *The Ultimate Collection,* with the energetic "(Love Is Like a) Heat Wave"

The Drifters: *Under the Boardwalk,* title song

We all love an evening at the beach, but if a quick train ride to Coney Island isn't on the travel itinerary for this summer or your Uncle Joe happens to be renovating the house down at the Jersey Shore, fear not. There are many ways to re-create the visual pleasures of an old beachside boardwalk that do not involve transportation by either subway or turnpike. Steven and Alexa told me after their party was over that they had never felt so relaxed as hosts. Of course, I like to take some credit, but I think the back-in-the-day vibe and cheerful colors were the real reason for their calm demeanor. Once again, I am reminded that we're all kids at heart — or even sun-burned teenagers, for that matter. So I'll never shy away from a few well-placed retro elements; they bring such happiness to people. If it means sneaking some lime freeze pops into a fabulous boat christening on the Long Island Sound, I'll take my chances.

JOIN US FOR A
SUMMER COCKTAIL PARTY
AS WE CHRISTEN OUR NEW BOAT
*Starry Nights*
MAY 28, 2004
SEVEN O'CLOCK IN THE EVENING
MUNIER'S DOCK
53 OPEN BAY DRIVE
REYNOLDS, NEW YORK

*Lisa & Allen Munier*

RSVP 516-342-0767

We're going overboard!

# Tutera Tips

1 Roll up colorful, large beach towels and use them as duffel pillows for the picnic area. You can reuse them as favors or as poolside towels for guests during the summer months.

2 Fill galvanized buckets with sand and use them to hold candles and snacks on tall skewers.

3 Remember that the correct height of the tables should be 30 inches for eating and 42 inches for cocktail tables; make sure your tablecloths are fitted accordingly.

4 Try making old-fashioned paper cone-shaped holders for your fries. Simply scan the pattern of your tablecloth and print out full-color 8½ x 11-inch pages. Roll the paper into cones, seal with a colorful sticker or clear tape, and fill with fries. This way your whole party will have a consistent look, from tablecloth to paper cones.

5 Create a one-of-a-kind serving tray by using old shutters and windowpanes. Remember, anything flat can be used to create levels for serving — so get creative!

6 Always be ready for unexpected weather when entertaining outside. Consider a tented area or make sure there is an indoor space nearby that is sufficiently decorated and ready to go in case of stormy conditions.

7 Try a self-service bar. There's something so simple and accommodating about a table of pre-mixed drinks ready for guests to snatch up as they enter the party.

8 Make sure your party is one to remember by creating a little mystery, such as a ride to the party on a newly christened boat.

9 When using an umbrella, make sure the base is securely weighted down using sandbags or bricks — especially by the water where wind is always an issue.

10 Create your own clothesline for pinning your cocktail napkins — simply string a line between two tree branches that are even in height.

# 2

## DINNER
## PARTIES

CABERNET AND CLOSE FRIENDS: A WINE-TASTING PARTY

YA-YA SISTERHOOD: AN OUTDOOR GARDEN PARTY

I've always imagined that somewhere, deep down, every party secretly longs to be a dinner party. They're so unabashedly celebratory: Why wait for a special day to pop up on the calendar when we have *dinner* to fete? For what seems like one of the most everyday kind of reason, we get to dress up and make merry with friends who intrigue and charm us. If you're looking for an intimate evening of laughter and conversation, nothing quite compares to the refined comforts of a dinner party at home. The best dinner parties seem to create this elegant sense of intimacy almost magically, out of some kind of effortless chemistry. While I totally believe in the power of magic — David Copperfield *did* date Claudia Schiffer for a while — it's precisely this illusion that requires careful consideration and planning. Luckily, after years of designing and attending dinner parties, I have a few tricks up my sleeve to help make this process as simple and rewarding as possible.

First things first. Even the most extravagant dinner parties begin at the beginning, with the humble guest list. Before you start planning the menu or the decor, you must know how many people you will be accommodating and who they are. Consider yourself the casting director of a fabulous production. Settle on a number of guests that will suit the scale of your kitchen's output and the number of diners you can seat around one table. As a basic rule, avoid multiple tables: the evening starts to feel more like a banquet, and inevitably, one table ends up as a castaway (and talking to a volleyball on a deserted island is just not glamorous in real life). After you've settled on a number, start balancing extroverted guests with less outgoing ones. And if you're not a big talker and storyteller, make sure you invite at least a couple of people who are; you'll be a guest, too. Once you've completed your list, send out official invitations with RSVPs that set the tone for the evening, like the wine-themed invitations I sent out for Nick and Karen Febrizio's wine-tasting party (see Tutera Tip #1, page 65). In a pinch, you *can* invite guests by phone in order to let your guests work around their own schedules, but this approach generates decidedly less mystery and anticipation.

With the guest list in hand, as well as an awareness of any reasonable dietary requirements, you can move confidently to the menu planning.

There are only a few fundamental rules here, and the most important of all is to avoid experimentation. Instead, do what you do best. Within this rule, there's plenty of room for creativity. I've served pigs-in-blankets at black-tie parties and paté at chic picnics. But the best menus foreground the freshest ingredients of the season without treading on the turf of holiday rituals. In other words, save the turkey for Thanksgiving Day. The second most important rule is to select a menu that can be prepared mostly in advance. This point is especially important if you don't have help in the kitchen. The only thing worse for a dinner party than the smell of burning is the sight of a frantic host shuttling from kitchen to living room with his or her face covered in flour. This is not relaxing. Plan out the timing of various courses in advance so you can spend time with your guests. Finally, serve dinner no more than one hour after everyone arrives, shooting for forty minutes as the ideal. Although your guests should have something to nibble on as soon as they get comfortable, and the pace of the meal should be leisurely, they should never feel like hostages to the promise of the next course; there is, after all, no subtle exit from an oppressively long salad course.

CONSIDER YOURSELF THE CASTING DIRECTOR OF A FABULOUS PRODUCTION.

It's only at this stage that you can begin to think about drinks. In general, I like to offer guests the option of a cocktail to start, and a selection of wine and nonalcoholic beverages suited to the menu. For many, the ritual of a simple, distinguished spirit can be the elegant detail that separates dining from eating. You can certainly mix a special batch of sangria or margaritas for an outdoor party in late summer, or offer sake as a prelude to a Japanese-inspired feast, but I tend to avoid creating multiple complicated theme-drinks for such occasions. Some understated specialty cocktails bring out the most in a meal, but classic cocktails like martinis and scotch on the rocks never fight with the flavors on the plate, and are wonderfully simple to prepare. In short, even a casual dinner party is not the place to act out Tom Cruise's scenes in *Cocktail.* Trust me, you'll have more time to enjoy your *own* cocktail.

Of course, one of the most essential things that *all* your guests should enjoy, whether or not they decide to indulge in a cocktail, is the decor. The best advice I can offer is to maximize the effects of minimal effort — you'll be busy. Focus attention largely on the spaces your guests will occupy: foyer, dining room, living room, and lest we forget, bathroom. Create a consistent mood that unifies the spaces through which the gathering will circulate, whether it's with a few candles and flowers, or with a rigorous design scheme. The most important thing you decorate, however, will be the table. Make this surface the heart of your party with a centerpiece or runner that keeps sight lines open and leaves room for serving dishes and, perhaps most importantly, save the intensely aromatic flowers for the powder room.

With all of these elements in place — guest list, menu, drinks, and decor — magical illusion of spontaneous charm should be within reach. At this point, it's up to you as the host, to quietly encourage mingling and spark conversations between guests, helping them circulate through the party. Depending on the formality and mood of your dinner party, you can achieve this effect in a number of different ways. For example, my friend

Star Jones likes to ask the men at her dinner parties to shift two seats to the right at each course to inspire new connections. When I work with Barbara Walters, she pays very close attention to her seating arrangements, making sure that any guest of honor is always seated to her immediate right. But whether you invigorate conversations by actively shaking up the mix or working behind-the-scenes, don't forget to sit back and marvel in enjoyment when the sound of laughter and conversation overwhelms the voice of the party planner in your head, because that's when the evening becomes truly magical.

Armed with this crash course in dinner party sleight of hand, you can confidently make even a simple meal worth remembering between friends. In the chapter that follows, I'll describe two of the most creative and enchanting affairs I've had the pleasure to stage: a genuine "Ya-Ya Sisterhood" garden dinner party, and a toasty, autumnal wine-tasting dinner party. You can re-create them in your own home or simply borrow your favorite ideas. And who knows? If you play your cards right, you might even meet a supermodel.

## CABERNET AND CLOSE FRIENDS: A WINE-TASTING PARTY
### for eight

When Nick and Karen Febrizio asked me to

PLAN A SMALL DINNER PARTY FOR A GROUP OF OLD FRIENDS

VISITING FROM OUT OF TOWN, I HAD A HEAD START. DESIGNING A

WEDDING FOR SOMEONE IS THE PARTY-PLANNING EQUIVALENT

OF READING THEIR DIARY — YOU LEARN WHO THEY ARE AND

WHAT MAKES THEM HAPPY — AND I HAD DESIGNED EVERY INCH

OF THE COUPLE'S NAPA NUPTIALS THE YEAR BEFORE.

SO I KNEW IN ADVANCE ABOUT THEIR PASSION (in the unauthorized biography, I'll call it an obsession) for good food and wine. Just attending tasting sessions for the reception menu, a smorgasbord of local fruits, cheeses, and wines required an extra thirty minutes on the treadmill every morning. Of course, it was all worth it: The outcome was a five-course extravaganza complete with some of the best wines the Mondavi vineyards had to offer. Naturally, the couple capped off the celebration with a honeymoon that took them on a wine-tasting tour of Europe.

Sitting in the living room of their Boston apartment once again while talking about food and wine as if we were back in Napa, I quickly realized that Nick and Karen had a similar extravaganza in mind. They wanted passion, fun, and the pleasures of the table to reign supreme, but they wanted someone else to help take care of the details while they spent a nice, long evening with their oldest friends; no panicking over the timing of a lovingly cooked meal or the decanting of a special port after dinner. It was a tricky situation: How could I create an equally sumptuous tribute to their love of dining that would uniquely suit the intimate scale of home? In the meantime, where was I going to find an extra thirty minutes for the gym?

Luckily, my memories of their lush wedding feast combined with the rich chestnut and rust color palette of their stately dining room inspired a solution to at least one of these challenges. My mind swirled with copper tones, candlelight, and lush roses — and that was *before* I started tasting wines for the big night.

These basic cues became essential to the character of the party — this was not a wedding dinner redux and I did not want to re-create Napa. So, instead of a pale, natural palette with lots of wildflowers, I opted for a little East Coast, old Bostonian flair in the form of deep burgundy hues and hints of gold. After dreaming up a floral table runner that brought true indulgence to Nick and Karen's dinner in the same rich wine-tinted tones, and incorporating a few souvenirs from their honeymoon, things started coming together. The two instantly fell in love with the idea of the decor and only the central task of the menu remained. Like all the best dinner parties, this one would not just feature one plate, one steak, and one potato, but a real multicourse progression of wine-and-food pairings. At such a leisurely tempo, Nick and Karen would have plenty of time to catch up with friends, and like the Europeans who first set this kind of slow pace, enough ballast to enjoy the next morning just as much.

### A ROOM FULL OF BLOOMS

I think of dining as a sensual revelation. As flavors shift and dance on the palate, we become ever more attuned to the environment around us. So, although Nick and Karen's modern burgundy-colored dining room presented a striking vision, the decorations for this elegant dinner party would have to capture the warmth, nuance, and romance of that sensuality in deep tones of wine and burnished, gold light. Undulating waves of coral-, merlot-, and copper-tinged roses, edged with tangles of grapes and deep green moss ran down the center of the table in a perfect tribute to the gentle hills of the Tuscan landscape. The chandelier was festooned with an abundance of grapes and leaves, connecting the feast to the Olympian rituals of dining that inspired it. Burgundy-, blue-, and copper-accented china played in the candlelight against burgundy- and midnight blue–rimmed crystal glasses. As if to bring all this alluring color and light into the earthly world of the vineyards, the look of wine bottles became a central theme: Decoupaged labels brought the feel of rustic wine country to the place cards, candle arrangements, lampshades, and invitations, while the corks of wines Nick and Karen had enjoyed in the past found new life as place-card holders and candle decorations. Who says that the contents of a wine bottle are all that matter?

### HOW TO

# Decoupage Glass Cylinders with Wine Labels

- Purchase a half dozen glass cylinders.

- Assemble plenty of your decoupage materials — in this case, used wine labels (but make sure they are not dark-colored).

- Apply a generous amount of Mod Podge (a decoupage glue) to each cylinder with a brush.

- Carefully paste the labels to cover the glass, overlapping at times.

- Smooth the surface with your brush and set aside to dry.

- Attach halved wine-bottle corks to the rim with a glue gun. (Corks are very lightweight, so they will stick easily.)

- Use small votives so that you can illuminate the whole cylinder, from top to bottom.

### WINE AND ROSES

In Greek mythology, wine and roses are inextricably linked. Rumor has it that Aphrodite gave the rose its beauty just by looking at it, while Dionysus gave it a sweet fragrance by "watering" its roots with wine. For Nick, Karen, and their guests, these two scents (and sentiments) would come together for one spectacular night, on one luxurious table. This runner, made of roses, is the epitome of elegant aromatherapy: one single flower in abundance, filling the room with a gentle perfume. Okay, so you're falling in love with this arrangement as you read these very words, but I know what you're thinking: "How can I make this at home?!" The answer is simple. Show the picture on the opposite page to your florist for some professional help, or make a slightly smaller arrangement yourself. It's not nearly as hard to assemble as it seems. And even better, it looks magnificent in all sizes, which works well for all wallets. I've created small versions for cocktail tables and enormous versions for long bridal tables or ballroom centerpieces; the number of compliments stays the same either way. You'll just need a few yards of plastic drop cloths, Oasis floral foam, and, of course, roses galore.

### HOW TO MAKE
## A Rosy Runner

- Cut three layers of plastic drop cloth in the shape of your centerpiece, leaving room at the edges.

- Mold oasis into low (1–3-inch) hills and valleys over the entire area, like the terrain of a golf course.

- Remove the oasis and soak it with just enough water so that it's moist, but not leaking.

- Return the wet oasis to the table and pin the edges of the plastic to the sides to prevent leakage.

- Add moss around the perimeter and in patterns across the surface of the oasis.

- Start adding cut roses (with 2–3-inch stems) to the mold until the entire surface is completely covered.

- Add bunches of red and purple grapes to the corners of the display, and voilà!

# The Touch

## VELVETY AND SMOOTH

The experience of tasting wine is all about subtlety and delicacy, and so were the textures that coaxed Nick and Karen's friends to appreciate every bit of the evening's culinary subtleties. From the soft, fragile rose petals, to the sleek finish of the crystal glasses, to the intricate etching of the fine china, every surface was light to the touch. Even the wine labels, which filtered lamp- and candlelight, were made of the most delicate paper. Likewise, the corks that rimmed them were of the most featherlight weight. Altogether, these textures set a refined but rustic tone for the meal to come, an atmospheric anticipation of what the night would hold.

## The Taste

### A DIONYSIAN DINNER MENU

Pairing great food with great wines is a must for any dinner party, but for this Dionysian evening of wine and roses I decided to indulge Nick, Karen, and their guests with a truly aphrodisiacal menu. In Dionysus's time, the officially "sexy" menu included basil, sage, pistachios, arugula, carrots, turnips, snails, "stink flesh" (a type of lizard), and lots and lots of wine.

Subtract the "stink flesh" (if only because you'll never find it at Whole Foods) and add some modern libido-friendly flavors — such as scallops, oysters, truffles, chocolate, and strawberries — and you've got a delicious grocery list. I wanted to create a sensual menu with luscious flavors, but not such an uber-romantic meal that they'd be embarrassed to serve it in front of company. We worked together to hit the right romantic note, and came up with what I like to call the "Dionysus Dinner Menu," which includes wine pairings for each course. We devoted so much time to getting it right that I felt it would be wrong to leave it out of this book. I have printed it and all the recipes in their entirety; consider it a love letter from wine country.

---

### Dionysus Dinner Menu

Courtesy of Fred Przyborowski of Restaurant Associates, Washington, D.C.

**FIRST COURSE**
CALIMYRNA FIGS
STUFFED WITH STILTON, BABY ARUGULA, DUCK PROSCUITTO, EXTRA-VIRGIN OLIVE OIL, AND AGED BALSAMIC VINEGAR

ROBERT MONDAVI, STAG'S LEAP DISTRICT, 2001 SAUVIGNON BLANC

**SECOND COURSE**
PAN-SEARED DIVER SCALLOPS
WITH WILD RICE, BUTTERNUT SQUASH, PECANS, AND A BLOOD ORANGE REDUCTION

ROBERT MONDAVI, CARNEROS DISTRICT, 2000 CHARDONNAY

**THIRD COURSE**
CINNAMON-CRUSTED COLORADO RACK OF LAMB WITH CELERIAC PUREE AND MANDARIN-MUSTARD JUS

ROBERT MONDAVI, 2000 CABERNET SAUVIGNON RESERVE

**FOURTH COURSE**
BANANA HAZELNUT CAKE
WITH SESAME BRITTLE ICE CREAM AND BUTTERSCOTCH SAUCE

ROBERT MONDAVI, 1999 SAUVIGNON BLANC BOTRYTIS

## CALIMYRNA FIGS
### STUFFED WITH STILTON, BABY ARUGULA, DUCK PROSCUITTO, EXTRA-VIRGIN OLIVE OIL, AND AGED BALSAMIC VINEGAR

*Serves 4*

1 pound baby arugula (cleaned thoroughly)

4 ounces duck prosciutto, sliced thin

4 ounces aged balsamic vinegar

8 ounces extra-virgin olive oil

4 strands of fresh chives

Salt and pepper to taste

FOR THE FIGS:

12 Calimyrna figs

8 ounces white wine

8 ounces sugar

8 ounces water

6–8 ounces Stilton blue cheese

12 pieces toasted brioche (about the size of a quarter)

Preheat oven to 325 degrees.

Remove tops of figs and simmer in pot using white wine, sugar, and water for 35 minutes, until tender. Strain and let cool.

Crumble blue cheese and stuff figs with it (it should look like the cheese is wearing a turban).

Heat stuffed figs in oven until warm; arrange in triangular fashion around plate atop toasted brioche.

### PLATING AND PRESENTATION

Dress arugula with olive oil and lightly season with salt and pepper. Gently place arugula in the center of the plate, between figs.

Roll prosciutto into a cigar shape and carefully tie each end with a chive. Drizzle with remaining olive oil and balsamic.

## PAN-SEARED DIVER SCALLOPS
WITH WILD RICE, BUTTERNUT SQUASH, PECANS, AND A BLOOD ORANGE REDUCTION

¼ cup butter

1 cup butternut squash, finely diced

½ cup pecans

½ cup shallots, minced

1 cup wild rice, cooked well until kernels split

½ cup cooked jasmine rice

8–12 u10 diver scallops (also called dry sea scallops)

1 bunch fresh chives, chopped

Blood Orange Reduction (see recipe, right)

Salt and pepper to taste


Start with a large sauté pan on med-low heat.

Melt butter, then add squash and cook just until tender. Add pecans and shallots, and cook for 1 minute.

Add wild rice and jasmine according to desired consistency and flavor.

Heat through, taste, and adjust seasonings.

While the rice stays warm, dry scallops with towel and remove membrane. Heat (heavy-duty) sauté pan on high until smoking. Add good quality cooking oil.

Quickly add diver scallops to pan, being careful not to overcrowd. Sear until dark brown on one side. Turn scallops over and do the same, or until scallops are medium rare. When finished, rest scallops on paper towel.

## BLOOD ORANGE REDUCTION

12 blood oranges

1 tablespoon whole-grain mustard

1 cup veal stock

¼ cup honey

1 sprig rosemary

1 shallot, chopped


Add all ingredients to sauce pot and reduce to syrup-like consistency.

### PLATING AND PRESENTATION

Sprinkle warm rice ragout with fresh chives and pack into mold or small cup. Invert on center of plate.

Arrange scallops around rice timbale and drizzle blood orange reduction around plate.

## CINNAMON-CRUSTED COLORADO RACK OF LAMB
### WITH CELERIAC PUREE AND MANDARIN-MUSTARD JUS

4 domestic frenched racks of lamb, 12 ounces each

4 ounces ground cinnamon

2 ounces ground ginger

2 ounces ground garlic

2 pounds celeriac (substitute parsnips if celeriac not available)

1 Idaho potato, peeled

2 cups heavy cream

4 ounces butter

Mandarin-Mustard Jus (see recipe, right)


Preheat oven to 350 degrees.

Rub lamb racks with mixture of cinnamon, ginger, and garlic.

Peel celery root and chop into small pieces.

Place celery root in small saucepan, add potato, heavy cream, and butter, and simmer until tender. (Make sure celeriac and potatoes are covered by liquid—if not, add a small amount of water.)

When tender, remove and reserve liquid. Add celery root mixture to food processor and puree. Add some of the cream and butter mixture back into food processor slowly. (You probably won't need all of the liquid.)

Grill lamb racks until browned. Finish in oven until about 125 degrees. Let rest for 10 minutes before slicing.


## MANDARIN-MUSTARD JUS

4 cups veal stock (beef or chicken stock works, too)

4 oranges, juiced

1 shallot, sliced thinly

Zest of one orange

¼ cup grain mustard

Salt and pepper to taste


Add all ingredients to sauce pot and reduce until sauce thickens to desired consistency. Season to taste.


## BANANA HAZELNUT CAKE
### WITH SESAME BRITTLE ICE CREAM AND BUTTERSCOTCH SAUCE

FOR SKILLET CAKE:

4 ounces butterscotch sauce (see recipe below)

2 bananas

1 cup heavy cream

½ cup eggs

¼ cup egg yolks

⅓ cup brown sugar

⅓ cup ground hazelnuts

2 tablespoons flour


Preheat oven to 325 degrees.

Place 1 ounce of butterscotch sauce in bottom of individual (small) Teflon cake pan.

Slice bananas and arrange over sauce, overlapping to cover bottom.

Mix all other ingredients in a separate bowl, pour on top of butterscotch and bananas, and bake for 20 minutes. Let cool 5 minutes.

## SESAME BRITTLE ICE CREAM

1 cup sugar

1 tablespoon water

1 tablespoon corn syrup

¼ cup black sesame seeds

1 pint premium vanilla ice cream, softened

Mix sugar in small saucepan with 1 tablespoon of water and the corn syrup; heat on high flame until amber. Make sure not to stir, shake, or wipe inside of pan before cooking so no sugar granules collect on walls of pan.

When sugar has turned amber you have caramel. Before it hardens too much, add sesame seeds, stir, and pour on to cookie sheet. Let cool until hard.

You will then have sesame brittle! After stealing a few bites, pulse brittle in food processor until crushed.

Fold crushed sesame brittle into ice cream (setting aside some for garnish) and refreeze until ready to use.

## BUTTERSCOTCH SAUCE

1½ cups brown sugar

¼ cup butter

Pineapple juice (substitute water, if necessary)

Add all ingredients in saucepan. Simmer until sugar dissolves.

## PLATING AND PRESENTATION

Invert warm banana cake on plate.

Drizzle with sauce and scoop ice cream on top. Garnish with sesame brittle and serve.

# Say Cheese!

FOR A PARTY REVOLVING AROUND WINE, don't forget the cheese board! This may sound like an old trick from your Aunty Mabel's treasure trove of 1950s party tips, but I've never seen a good selection of cheeses go unnoticed. In fact, nothing elevates the sophistication of a postprandial reverie quite like the variety of flavors it offers. Stop by the cheese department at your local gourmet supermarket and ask for selections that include at least one to strike the palate (like a bleu or a sharp cheddar), one to soothe it (like a triple-cream brie or any mellow cow's milk cheese), and one to intrigue it (like an aged sheep's milk cheese or an unusual goat cheese). At home, pair each of the cheeses with an accompaniment. You can either follow your instincts or ask for advice at the shop, but I love goat cheese with wild berries and slivered almonds baked over brie. Any way you slice it, these luxuriant, rich flavors will inspire your guests to savor each sweet in a completely new way.

# Pairing Food and Wine

NICK AND KAREN CAN BE CONSIDERED lucky. They had a carefully selected list of wines from the Mondavi Estate just waiting to find their culinary counterparts, but not all of us are always so prepared. Finding the perfect wine to go with a meal is one of those little things that makes a huge difference, though. In dining, as in life, when the marriage between the two is a good one, they *both* benefit. After all, a dinner party focused on wine is much less likely to turn out like *The Lost Weekend* if your guests take the time to consider the flavors in play. Of course, I won't lie to you — a lot can go into selecting the right wine for a dish, from understanding the agricultural output of a particular wine region, to considering what kind of oak casks held the wine before it was bottled.

But here's the good news: Even if you don't feel like getting the long version from your local wine merchant or learning all about exciting topics like botrytis, "the noble rot" that gives Sauternes their depth, there are a few basic rules you can follow to make an ideal match. First, decide whether you want the wine to act as a contrast or as an echo to the flavors and textures of the food; either one can work well. For instance, pair a rich fish like salmon with a crisp and acidic dry Riesling to lighten the palate, or with a juicy red Zinfandel that can offer just as much flavor, and heighten the sensation of the sweet, velvety texture. Second, consider the fruits you might like to taste alongside a certain meal. Do you want something citrusy, like lemons and oranges? Or bright and sweet, like raspberries and cherries? Or dark and sweet, like blackberries and figs? Look for wines with descriptions that match these fruit profiles. The closest thing to a bottom line is to make sure that the flavors of the food don't totally overwhelm those of the wine or vice versa. Most important, have fun. After all, what could be more fun than simply tasting a series of different wines to see where your intuition leads you?

# The Sound

For many people the most comforting sound in the world consists of laughter and the clinking of wine glasses as they and their guests toast one another. So, as a background to the chiming of glasses I played some of the Febrizio's wedding songs (not the DJ dance numbers, but the cocktail instrumental numbers) from a series of mixed CDs I had burned for the occasion. I could spend days on iTunes, mixing CDs for parties. You can buy any song you want for ninety-nine cents. It's like having your dream jukebox at your disposal. If you don't have a teenage kid to help explain to you the simple procedure for CD burning, you can always simply select your five favorite albums and put them on rotation for the night's play list. Here's a list of the ones I would choose for such a party:

Andrea Bocelli: *Romanza*

Rosemary Clooney: *16 Most Requested Songs,* "Mambo Italiano"

Josh Groban: *Closer,* "You Raise Me Up"

Marlene Dietrich: *Falling in Love Again,* "You Go to My Head"

Loston Harris: *Comes Love*

Antonio Vivaldi: *The Four Seasons*

Johannes Brahms: *Symphonies No. 3 and 4*

At the end of the night, when Nick and Karen gave each of their guests a bottle of their favorite wine from their honeymoon haul, it occurred to me how enduring the memory of a good dinner party can be. Sure, those of us who get carried away with the pleasure of food, drink, and conversation may feel light-headed whether or not we overindulge. But the complete sensual experience of a properly adorned table and a meal prepared with love and imagination ages almost as well as a good bottle of Burgundy.

1 Create a small gift box with your invitation: Purchase a box with a lid designed to hold a photograph, add your invitation here and enclose a little gift inside, hinting at the festivities to come. In this case, we sent a wick wine-bottle topper so that guests could transform an empty wine bottle into a new — yet old-fashioned-looking — lantern.

2 As a parting gift, offer each guest a bottle of dessert wine housed in a wooden box filled with merlot-colored tissue and decorated with decoupaged labels. You can even use a wine label as the gift-card enclosure.

3 Substitute inexpensive paper lampshades for your permanent ones and decoupage them with wine labels to create a charming, rustic glow of light.

4 Decoupage plain napkin rings with vintage wine labels to coordinate each place setting with the overall look.

5 Use two corks (with slits cut down their sides) as place-card holders.

6 Develop a relationship with a good local wine seller. Once you establish a rapport, these wine lovers will be endlessly helpful with tips and will sometimes offer discounts, too!

7 Serve each round of new wine in a new glass. Make sure, too, that the glass is the appropriate shape and size for the wine.

8 Do not fill wine glasses to the rim. For a tasting like this, pour each glass about a third full. For large red-wine glasses, only a quarter of the glass should be filled.

9 At any dinner party where wine is a central element, make sure there is always food within reach, especially at the beginning of the night. No guest should be expected to drink more than a few sips of alcohol without accompaniment.

10 Remove wine-bottle labels by coating them with a thick layer of peanut butter and letting the goop-covered bottle sit overnight. In the morning, rinse the bottle and the label will easily peel off.

## YA-YA SISTERHOOD: AN OUTDOOR GARDEN PARTY

*for six*

The prospect of an outdoor dinner party can

BE DAUNTING. SOMEHOW A PEACEFUL BACKYARD SUDDENLY

SEEMS TO HOLD A CAPACITY FOR TRULY BIBLICAL VENGEANCE

TOWARD CIVILIZATION. NERVOUS HOSTS ENVISION BLISTERING

HEAT, SWARMS OF WINGED INSECTS, DAYS AND NIGHTS

OF RAIN, OR PERHAPS EVEN A SCENE FROM *THE BIRDS*.

BUT THE TRUTH IS, WITH THE RIGHT KIND OF PLANNING

AND ATTENTION, AN OUTDOOR DINNER PARTY CAN BE

POSITIVELY MAGICAL AND SURPRISINGLY MANAGEABLE.

THE REAL TRICK IS TO COME TO TERMS with what I like to call the Hoover Dam principle: Work with nature, not against it. Dining outside is not just for the paper-plate set, where every feast must be movable and disposable, and the only perfume is OFF! bug spray. On the contrary, it is at its finest when the trappings of the great indoors — from fine china to linen napkins — find harmony with the caprice of the landscape.

As a party planner, sometimes the most challenging part of designing an outdoor dinner is convincing clients of how deeply memorable a good one can be. But when I suggested the idea to Jo Ann Atwood, who wanted to treat her five very dearest friends to something more meaningful than yet another rib roast, she instantly understood why nothing else would do. Either she'd been to the Hoover Dam and learned her lesson, she read my mind, or she simply knew that friendships like hers would be right at home in a garden. In the fifty years since they all met in grade school in Atlanta, the bond among these friends took root and grew through weddings, divorces, and more weddings; raising children and spoiling new grand-children; following careers, dreams, and one another. They meet regularly for tea and vacation together when it's been too long between visits, and each year, one of them throws a celebratory dinner for the others. This year it was Jo Ann's turn and she wanted the evening to serve as a gift express-ing the essence of their friendships. And for true "Ya-Ya Sisterhood," I couldn't imagine a more fitting gift than staging a slow-paced Southern-style feast in Jo Ann's lush countryside backyard, an often underused setting that could easily be transformed into their own secret garden, which they might very well need given how many bad hairdos, doomed crushes, and hilariously embarrassing stories they'd cultivated over the years.

The party that grew out of this initial idea not only pays perfect trib-ute to this remarkable group of ladies, it represents all of the best things an outdoor dinner party can be for any occasion: a truly harmonious moment between excitement and relaxation, the organic and the ceremonious, the unexpected and the unforgettable. With the clever use of a cherished urn from the garden and a few favorite sun hats, several lengths of chiffon in the soft, sweet colors of the late spring garden blooming all around the table, and a smattering of sparkling butterflies to beckon the group back to girlhood, the distinction between centerpiece and natural peace would be gloriously blurred. The easy pace of the meal, which marries the home-grown flavors of real Southern cooking with some of the loftier delicacies of teatime, would also give the six friends plenty of time to trade stories, crack wise, and enjoy the fruits of a well-tended friendship. In fact, by the time they would move to the dessert table, which took them to a fresh corner of the garden, I felt certain next spring's tall tales were already planted.

# The Look

## MY SECRET GARDEN

If you read *The Secret Garden* as a child, you might recall the central message: Time spent in a beautiful garden can cure you of all ailments, both in body and in mind. When I plan a garden party, I like to remember this message and make sure to draw the garden out as much as dress it up. When decorating for Jo Ann, I focused on matching the beautiful vistas in her garden with complementary motifs from the dining room or, in some cases, from my party-planning bag of tricks. The beauty of Jo Ann's blossoming rose garden was inspiration for the pastel chiffon fabric, delicate floral and butterfly patterns on the china, and silk rose petals attached to each napkin. Small butterfly salt-and-pepper shakers, rhinestone butterfly figurines around the bouquet, butterfly-shaped napkin holders, and white chocolate butterfly garnishes on the lemon cakes echoed the real butterflies already fluttering around the garden. The twinkle of midnight stars gave me the idea to blanket the setting with flickering candlelight. Even the landscape of the garden served as a template for the dinner party layout: Just as it extends deeply into the woods, with nooks and crannies at every turn, this party would extend well into the evening with dinner in one tucked-away area and dessert in another secret spot. The message of this story: Start with your reality and use imagination to build your version of paradise from it. Soon, you may have the cure for all ailments, too.

# The Scent

### LEMONS AND LILACS

As much as I love the smoky aroma of mesquite (or even the promising waft of burning lighter fluid on a summer afternoon), this outdoor party was not about the scent of briquettes and barbecue sauce. No, this party was all about the crisp, clean fragrance of a spring garden after a good rainfall. I wanted these women to feel energized by scents of lemon zest, lilacs, roses, and a spring lawn. We cut the grass, raked, and watered everything in sight the day before the party. We ironed the table linens with a mist of fresh rose water and placed rose-scented candles in the powder room. At the table, fragrant roses and potent lilacs filled the air with gentle perfume. To add a zing of citrus to the meal, fresh lemon and clementine wedges were used as a garnish for the water glasses and lemon bundt cake was served for dessert. Throughout the meal, the scent of green garden freshness came in the form of pert cucumbers, crisp radishes, mixed spring greens, and citrus-lime dressing. I'm sure it was more than these mingling, energetic aromas that kept these ladies talking well into the night, but they most definitely didn't hurt.

# The Touch

## WEIGHTLESS AS A BUTTERFLY WING

In an effort to match nature's own cool, smooth textures — think rich moss, downy spring grass, and weightless butterfly wings — I decorated the entire dinner party with soft frayed linens, light chiffon, delicate spring flowers, and lots of silk rose petals. I wanted everything to feel soft and light, gentle and comforting. After all, a ladies' garden party should feel as essentially feminine to the touch as it does to the soul. Even the table was a tribute to the texture of rich, velvety moss. I found a moss-covered urn Jo Ann had hidden deep in her garden. It was an extraordinary vessel, straight out of *Midnight in the Garden of Good and Evil,* and when used as the base for the dining table, evidence that sometimes your party decor can begin "right in your own backyard." We weighed down the urn with bricks to ground it, and then topped it with a sixty-inch glass tabletop. (Note: This urn was over twenty-four-inches wide, broad enough to balance the glass table with no risk of tipping. If your base is less than twenty-four-inches, revise your plans.) The smooth glass over the rustic urn imitated the textures of creek water over mossy stones. To expand this sensation even further, I added textures of soft flower petals to almost every detail: silk flowers for the cushions and napkins, roses attached to sun hats, petals gathered into small wrought-iron baskets, and an overflowing bouquet of roses, lilac, lily of the valley, and peonies for the table. For the dessert table, I used a frayed linen tablecloth and napkins to add softness to the formality of fine Ann Weatherly china and crystal glasses. Finally, I attached yards of silky chiffon fabric to broad-brimmed sun hats and casually hung them on each chair back.

## HOW TO MAKE
# Flower Cushions

THESE CUSHIONS are so simple to make that I *must* encourage you to take a crack at them. We used Jo Ann's wrought-iron garden chairs, but any garden chair will do.

- Purchase six very basic waterproof garden chair cushions and enough silk petals to cover all of them.

- Using a hot glue gun or needle and thread, attach the petals to the cushions. Begin at the edges of the cushions and work inward.

- Avoid creating a circular pattern by arranging the petals in a haphazard design. The goal is for the petals to look as if they were thrown up in the air before landing on the cushion.

## LIGHT AND CRISP

If a perfect afternoon in the garden has a culinary equivalent, it is surely the tea sandwich. In the cool, smooth crunch of thinly sliced cucumbers, the luscious veneer of homemade mayonnaise, the spicy smattering of watercress, the neat slices of dense, white sandwich bread shorn of its crust, and the faintest hint of salt and pepper, you can taste the essence of delicacy; it is fresh, enlivening, and soothing in its simplicity. There may be nothing ladylike about the way I've seen grown men jealously hoard trays of them, but I knew Jo Ann's evening with her girlfriends would not be complete without them, especially because they have all philosophized on the perfect tea sandwich over long afternoons together.

The light, refreshing course of tea sandwiches served in a hollowed loaf of bread was just an introduction to the array of similarly delicate flavors that would define the evening. For the menu as a whole I adapted garden-fresh produce to the lighter demands of the summer appetite, which allowed for the ladies to chat while tasting the finger sandwiches. Each lady was then presented with a lobster salad wrapped in cucumber slices and topped with mixed greens drizzled in citrus dressing. For the main course, Jo Ann and her guests dined on braised halibut with lemon and capers, and escarole and corn succotash. The soft, mild flavor of the fish blended with the bright zing of citrus and the briny capers in a quiet symphony of elemental flavors, while the bitter escarole and the sweet corn achieved a natural balance befitting the scene around the table. A lemon bundt cake as sweet and bright as sunshine offered the evening's final flutter but, just as a garden finds its fragile beauty in the organic whole, the larger combination of subtle, natural ingredients created a casual kind of extravagance for the diners.

# The Sound

When the guest list is only six people long, you might imagine a little background music would help to liven the atmosphere. However, when the guest list is six *best friends* long, the atmosphere is plenty livened just by howls of laughter and overlapping banter. I figured additional sound effects need only "chime in" between giggle fits, so I purchased six wind chimes to hang from the wisteria in the garden. Chimes work beautifully for this kind of garden party, adding subtle background music as well as a nice decorative touch. At the end of the evening, Jo Ann asked each of her guests to pick one of the hanging wind chimes to take home. From now on, every time the wind blows, each of these ladies will be reminded of their friendship.

Of course, as subtle and perfect as the chimes were, I must confess that I couldn't resist a little extra DJ intervention. A few weeks before the party I asked Jo Ann for a list of songs she and her friends had enjoyed over the years. She rattled off a long list of songs guaranteed to send these ladies reeling down memory lane. I set about the business of making custom CDs. When I handed them to Jo Ann on the afternoon of the party, I suggested that she pop them in only after a good round of cocktails (and memories) had been stirred. Whether cued or simply pulled out when the mood seems right, homemade soundtracks are always a huge hit when old friends reunite. There's nothing as fun or funny as a few musical reminders of years gone by. Here are some of my favorites:

Bette Midler: *Divine Collection,* "Friends" and "Miss Otis Regrets"

Reba McEntire: *Greatest Hits,* Vol. 2

*Practical Magic* soundtrack, which includes songs by Stevie Nicks and Joni Mitchell, among others

Shania Twain: *Come on Over*

Linda Ronstadt: *The Very Best of Linda Ronstadt,* "Blue Bayou"

Annie Lennox: *Diva,* "Keep Young and Beautiful"

Ella Fitzgerald: *The First Lady of Song,* "A-Tisket, A-Tasket"

The Andrews Sisters: *Cocktail Hour,* "Hold Tight (Want Some Seafood, Mama)"

I won't lie to you. I've sat through my share of movies about delicately tough, eccentric southern women, from *Gone with the Wind* to *Steel Magnolias.* Well, Jo Ann and her friends are the real deal, so let's just say I was a little curious — just a *little* — about whether or not Vivien Leigh and Julia Roberts got the story straight. Yes, it made me a little nervous that my ears were burning through long stretches of the evening. And, yes, when a dark cloud threatened the salad course, I heard Jo Ann declare the occasion for a rain dance all the way from the house, and the six of them laughing uproariously as the cloud quickly (coincidentally?) passed. Chalk one up for Julia. But the movies could never do justice to the familiarity and affection that radiated from the corners of the garden where the real sisterhood held court. At the end of the evening, when Jo Ann asked each guest to remember the unique feeling of the garden that night by picking out one of the wind chimes, which whispered a soundtrack to their gathering, I have to admit I felt a warmth beyond Hollywood's reach.

# Tutera Tips

1  When the majority of your guests fall in the same age group, play music that is most fitting to that generation. It will stir memories and inspire great conversations.

2  If you feel like your table is missing something, it probably is. Try adding small details, like rose petals, strands of ribbon, or small pieces of faux jewelry, such as rhinestones or fake pearls, to the table.

3  There is nothing more elegant than proper tea service. To make a royal impression, forgo the standard bagged tea leaves and, instead, use high-quality loose tea leaves. Start the brewing process with fresh, cold water and, once it boils, transfer it to your favorite teapot and strainer for table service.

4  Attach several hanging plants to overhead branches to create a floral canopy over an outdoor dining area.

5  Rather than asking each guest to RSVP by phone, ask each friend to send you an old photo to let you know she (or he) will be attending your party. By putting each photo in a beautiful frame, you can create a unique place card.

6  To add a little theatricality and an element of surprise, serve dinner in one area and dessert in another.

7  For a unique napkin treatment, sew silk rose petals to the edges of beige- or pink-colored cloth napkins. Tie with ribbon and, presto — you have created individual bouquets for each guest.

8  For a unique style of serving food, hollow the center of a fresh loaf of bread and fill the space with tea sandwiches and small fruits and vegetables.

9  It's a good idea to leave open areas in a yard for butterflies to sun themselves, as well as partly shady areas so they can hide when it's cloudy or cool off when it's hot. The same goes for your guests.

10  When attending an outdoor party, bring a gift for the garden. A baby tree or a baby rosebush always makes a beautiful contribution to your host's garden and it will remind them of you every time they admire it.

$3$

# HOLIDAY ENTERTAINING

Something special happens during holidays. Suddenly, in the middle of an otherwise ordinary string of days, we all share the excitement of celebration. Everyone does their part in making the places we live, work, and play just a little more festive, and the bonds that unite us just a little more meaningful. On the Fourth of July, the scent of mesquite and burning sparklers curls through every backyard gathering. After dark, picnic blankets unfurl as we all watch the same gorgeous display of fireworks — and who can deny the experience? Nothing makes me feel more connected to the people around me than that gleam in all of our eyes as we finish our last errands on Christmas Eve, stopping to admire the decorated storefronts, the lights, the holly, and the carols. Even the grumpy old cat at my favorite flower shop doesn't seem to mind wearing a tiny red bow on this one occasion. Not for a minute or two, anyway.

More than anything else, traditions are the touchstones that make holidays this source of communal joy. We all feel a thrill when the first pumpkin vendor sets up shop in October, just as we do when the first champagne bottle pops on New Year's Eve. It's not because the sensation is unexpected, but because it returns us to the moments of happiness that we all experience when we are together. That's why I almost never budge on one fundamental rule of holiday entertaining: Always begin with tradition. Thanksgiving is known as "Turkey Day" for a reason, so unless you're hosting a room full of vegetarians, do not disappoint the tribe of the drumstick. The same goes for decorations. I've seen even the most blasé hipsters positively *sink* on arrival at a Christmas party that was too chic to show its tinsel. After all, the word "holiday" comes from "holy day," and even though many of our holidays are secular now, their underlying sense of ritual is no less important to respect.

Of course, that doesn't mean you can't put a new spin on a classic idea. In my experience, the stunning theatricality of the holidays — their ceremony, playfulness, and splendor — brings out the creative genius in all of us. Bachelors who shun the kitchen obsessively tend to simmering pots of their own special chili on Super Bowl Sunday. Workaholics scamper around their apartments searching for a striking lighting scheme for an intimate Valentine's Day dinner, or just the right balance of flavors for a new variation on the same old mashed potatoes. Why not put a few brave new ideas on display with the essentials?

I tweaked the rules for each of the three holiday parties that follow, and I encourage you to do the same. For instance, instead of climbing onto the typical bandwagon of Christmas hors d'oeuvres parties, invite your friends to a late evening "Crystal Christmas Dessert Party" (page 103). Or, next Halloween, breathe a sophisticated but whimsical new life into the ghost of parties past by emphasizing the storied charms of the season over the normal trappings of trick-or-treat. The "Harvest Moon: An Autumnal Party" (page 87) will give you a cornucopia of ideas to make a simple October dinner magical and invigorating. But maybe you want something more. Maybe you want to celebrate an altogether different kind of holiday, to explore and interpret another culture's traditions. Then take a page from my "Chinese New Year Party" (page 119), and rest assured that the coming Year of the Rooster will bring you a wealth of unforgettable parties. Have fun with them. For all of the holiday parties I design, including the ones you will see in the following pages, I try to invoke the sense of wonder and play that we all felt as children during holiday festivities, but without forgetting the more cultivated pleasures of the grown-up world. It's this peculiar blend of youth and experience, comfort and revelation, past and future, that makes the holidays so sublime, and if you can capture it, your friends and family could want no greater gift.

When I was growing up, I looked forward to

HALLOWEEN THE WAY THAT OTHER KIDS LOOKED FORWARD TO

THE LAST DAY OF SCHOOL OR TO THEIR BIRTHDAYS. MY MOTHER

NEVER LET A HALLOWEEN GO BY WITHOUT THRILLING US WITH

TREATS AND SURPRISES. THESE DAYS, I LEAVE THE TRICK-OR-

TREATING TO THE LITTLE ONES, BUT THERE IS STILL NOTHING I

LOVE MORE THAN PLANNING A GREAT HALLOWEEN BASH. LET ME

GET ONE THING STRAIGHT, THOUGH: I AM NOT TALKING ABOUT

DRY ICE, PLYWOOD COFFINS, OR BOWLS FULL OF CANDY CORN.

ESPECIALLY AT HOLIDAY PARTIES that are conventionally thrown for kids, it is important to remember the crucial difference between making your guests *feel* like kids and *treating* them like kids. Stick your hand in a bowl of peeled-grape "eyeballs" on your way through a friend's "haunted house," and you will know, better than you could ever want to, the very essence of this difference. But there is a solution. As I discovered while savoring the Halloween nights of my youth, holidays like this one are as much about the season as they are about the rituals, and especially as we outgrow those capes and masks, they should be celebrated accordingly.

For "Harvest Moon: An Autumnal Party," it was precisely this seasonal mood that I tried to capture. Over a fuzzy cell phone signal several continents away, Valerie Shaw, a globe-trotting news producer, asked me to design a Halloween event for her and her husband Mike's friends and colleagues. She wanted something that would indulge her nostalgia for the playfulness of the occasion, but also make up for all the gorgeous autumn evenings at home she'd missed in more recent years while on assignment.

HOLIDAYS LIKE THIS ONE ARE AS MUCH ABOUT THE SEASON AS THEY ARE ABOUT THE RITUALS.

Like myself, Valerie had a soft spot for Halloween; she admitted to keeping Wonder Woman cuffs and her golden lasso of truth in the attic. But what excited her more was the anarchic energy of playing in the leaves as a child, aromatic spices carried on high winds, and the crackling warmth of a bright hearth. So, with these Halloween delights in mind, I designed an intimate, rustic dinner party for eight. It started with an invitation printed on a card and attached to a tube filled with dried pumpkin seeds. This truly planted the "seed" for the feeling of the party. Richly colored arrays of autumn leaves, grapevines, and bittersweet on the mantel, the iron wall sconces, and even the dining room table brought the whimsical charms of the outdoors in; pumpkins of all sizes filled with cinnamon, anise, and glowing candles lit up a feast for the senses; burnished tones of amber and rough-hewn swags of burlap and plaid put a playful kind of farmhouse-rococo finish on the whole scene. That night, the neighborhood kids got all the candy, but Valerie, Mike, and their guests savored their own special treat.

# The Look

Autumn is such a magnificent season to look at: Trees are ablaze with amber, gold, and crimson, skies are a clear, crisp blue, and front porches are adorned with orange pumpkins. Of course, it was just a little too cold on October 31 to bring Valerie and Mike's guests outside, so it became my job to bring autumn's colors inside. I began my decor list, as always, with a nod toward tradition: pumpkins, dried leaves, gourds, cinnamon, berries, and dried corn. Then I brought in a few complementary elements, such as raw burlap, wood bushels, chartreuse silk, pale green candles, and orange tartan. Finally, I chose rust-colored plates, olive green and amber glasses, and coiled copper flatware.

Once I had assembled these basics it was just a matter of time (and a little party-planning insanity) before the Shaws' Connecticut dining room was transformed into a virtual pumpkin patch. I had to clear a few naysay-

ers from the room as I started lining the table with leaves, but to their great surprise, the leaves worked as a wonderful decoration without cluttering the place-settings and serving area. I carved low-relief patterns onto the surfaces of two big, beautiful pumpkins. The patterns (winding vine and leaf motifs) made for a subtle and grown-up alternative to the jack-o-lantern. I created place cards from burlap-edged wood, and accented them with an orange plaid fabric. The centerpiece was one of my favorite innovations, though: It wasn't just on the table! The same motif of cinnamon and candle-filled pumpkins alongside bouquets of dried leaves and berries extended to the mantel (it's not just for Christmas), chandelier, and sconces. The warm fire and candlelight was key, if a bit risky (see my tip on candles and dried leaves, page 101), as it cast a lovely flickering of light over the whole scene. By the time I started tightening the chartreuse silk-lined burlap "corsets" on the dining room chairs, my vision was assembled to perfection and the Shaws were ready to entertain.

## HOW TO MAKE
# Burlap-Covered Chairs

THIS IS SO EASY TO DO. Just remember that it's a "rustic" look.

- Cover the seat of each chair with burlap. Pin it under the seat to secure it.

- Wrap more burlap around the seat back and use garden twine to lace the two edges together, starting at the top. You do not need to create holes for the lacing as the twine will thread through the loose weave of the burlap.

- Slide a piece of green dupioni silk fabric behind the laced twine and pin into place.

# The Scent

## WHAT'S COOKING?

Just as the smell of a great summer barbecue can draw people out of the house, the smell of a classic autumn roast can keep them in. Part of creating a sumptuous, mouthwatering atmosphere at a fall or winter party can be as simple as cracking the kitchen door. At this harvest meal, I made sure that all of my carefully selected savory aromas would spill out into the house and woo guests the moment they arrived. Later, around the dinner table, the aromatic combination of decanted red wine, burning logs on the fire, and fresh sticks of cinnamon, anise, and cloves — displayed in miniature carved pumpkins — had them all reeling with delight. As the midnight hour approached, everyone seemed so contented I thought they might melt into their chairs if I didn't send one last strategic message from beyond the kitchen door: the waft of percolating coffee.

## CRISP LEAVES UNDERFOOT

I love the bristly feel of dried leaves and scratchy burlap as much as the next guy but, let's face it, these are not textures one easily associates with dinner-party elegance. However, there is a way to integrate these quintessentially autumnal surfaces into your decor without rubbing your guests the wrong way. Balance rough surfaces with smooth ones, such as soft dupioni silk (used to line the chair covers, pumpkin-bread wrapping, napkins, and tablecloth), sleek wine glasses, and shiny wax candles. Then you won't have to worry about roughing it.

## HOW TO CREATE
### A Leaf Tablecloth

- Begin with any ready-made tablecloth or a few yards of fabric (it doesn't matter whether the edges are finished or not). Try using an orange-colored fabric — if the material shows through, it will blend in with the color of the leaves.

- Starting at the outside edges of the cloth, glue the leaves (using a glue gun), allowing for a slight overlap. Continue row by row until you reach the center.

NOTE: There's no way to "mess it up." Just make sure you have a ton of leaves.

# The Taste

The Shaws' dinner guests got to savor their first taste of the harvest dinner to come without even leaving their houses. I attached plastic spice tubes filled with freshly roasted pumpkin seeds to each invitation. But I didn't stop there. I figured if you're going to let your guests nosh on party snacks before the party has started, why not give them something to nibble on the day after? Valerie and Mike offered small loaves of pumpkin bread (along with the family recipe) as parting favors. In between all this yummy snacking, I served up a hearty fall feast of butternut squash soup (garnished with chives and blue cheese and served in carved-out acorn squash), followed by duck braised with red wine and figs alongside roasted polenta, grilled carrots, and baby squash. For dessert, I offered open-faced apple tart, cinnamon-sprinkled ice cream, and roasted chestnuts. The key for picking a menu in the late fall is to select seasonal flavors without duplicating Thanksgiving classics, such as sweet potatoes, cranberry sauce, stuffing, and pumpkin pie. Even die-hard turkey fans can tire of the tasty bird after a month of leftover sandwiches. Let's face it, if you start your party with pumpkin seeds and end with pumpkin bread, you can save your pumpkin pie for November.

## PUMPKIN BREAD

*Makes 3 loaves. Prep time: 15 minutes*

1 can (29 ounces) Libby's 100% Pure Pumpkin

4 eggs

1 cup Crisco oil

⅓ cup water

1 teaspoon vanilla

2 tablespoons pumpkin-pie spice

2 tablespoons allspice

2 tablespoons cinnamon

1 tablespoon ground nutmeg

3½ cups flour

3 cups sugar

2 teaspoons baking soda

1 teaspoon salt

sugar/water glaze (dissolve ¼ cup sugar in warm water)

Combine pumpkin, eggs, oil, water, vanilla, and spices and mix well, either by hand or with an electric mixer.

Sift together flour, sugar, baking soda, and salt and add to pumpkin mixture. Blend well.

Either grease and flour 3 (8 x 3 ¾ x 2 ½–inch) foil pans, or spray them with Pam (butter or original flavor). Pour mixture into loaf pans.

Bake at 350 degrees for 1 hour and 20 minutes or until a toothpick comes out clean from the center of each loaf.

Let loaves stand about 5 minutes. Remove the warm loaves from the pans and brush the top of each loaf with the sugar/water glaze. Once cooled, refrigerate.

Serve with butter, ice cream, or whipped cream or toast bread in a toaster oven with butter.

# The Sound

The wind whistling through the dry branches outside might be a nice sound effect as guests walk up your driveway, but once inside you can supplement nature's music with a little help from your home stereo. For a festive holiday feast, standard dinner party music rules apply: Keep the music instrumental and in the background, but don't forget to play any music at all! A quiet dining room can startle people and freeze conversation (needless to say, a boom box pumping out Michael Jackson's "Thriller" will have a similar effect). We opted for a little of Valerie's favorite country music artists (Shania Twain, Alan Jackson, Garth Brooks, and Martina McBride) to play through dinner. These heart-warming songs resonated even more in this rustic, "country" setting. Here are some suggestions:

Andy Williams: *Moon River & Other Movie Themes,* "Moon River"

Martha Raye: *Here's Martha Raye,* "Peter, Peter Pumpkin Eater"

John Mayer: *Room for Squares*

Neil Young: *Harvest Moon*

Carole King: *Tapestry,* "You've Got a Friend"

Tim McGraw: *Set This Circus Down*

As a gutsy and ambitious news producer, Valerie Shaw knows how to keep her finger on the pulse of a breaking story, but she never anticipated getting "scooped" on the frolicking fun of her very own dinner party. Before she and Mike had even run through all the pleasures of sharing their autumn bounty with the people in their lives, their small town was buzzing with talk about her playful take on seasonal decor, the striking menu of autumn flavors, and the possible secrets of her family recipe for pumpkin bread. Valerie was, of course, tickled pink to be at the center of such impassioned reports on the state of entertaining in her hometown. But the feeling that sustained her, even after she returned to work on the other side of the world, was the thrilling hope of playing in the leaves with friends for many Halloweens to come.

# Tutera Tips

1 When using fresh vegetables as decor on your table or mantel, rub them lightly with vegetable oil to bring out their vibrant colors and to add a soft sheen.

2 To keep pumpkins fresh, store them in a cool, dry, and dark area — but do not freeze them.

3 Use a serrated knife when carving your pumpkin — it is much easier and safer than a regular knife.

4 Hollow out squash or miniature pumpkins to serve a first-course soup or even a pumpkin ice cream or mousse for dessert.

5 When hollowing out your pumpkin, save the seeds for roasting: They are great to add to granola, ice cream, or even to salt and eat by themselves.

6 Use inexpensive fabric, such as burlap, to cover chairs or even your buffet table. Cut and fray the edges to create a more rustic and natural look.

7 When using burlap for a decorative element, wash and dry the fabric (using the "delicate" setting on your washing machine) to soften the material and the edges.

8 Use artificial or dried floral elements for areas such as your mantel or when decorating a chandelier, which makes especially good use of items like branches, vines, and bittersweet. High-quality items look so realistic that you will have to touch them to tell the difference!

9 When your party is over, gently roll (do not fold) your tablecloth of dried leaves with a single layer of tissue paper (white, not colored) and store for next year.

10 Try using fresh fruits and vegetables as decor elements. When your party is over, use them to make fresh soups and/or smoothies, or even cut them into cubes and freeze them for future cooking.

## CRYSTAL CHRISTMAS:
## A DESSERT PARTY
*for twenty*

Every year when the holiday season rolls

AROUND, WE COUNT ON CERTAIN THINGS GETTING STUFFED:

STOCKINGS, TURKEYS, AND BELLIES. BUT ONE KIND OF STUFFING

THAT ALWAYS SEEMS TO SNEAK UP ON US IS THE KIND THAT

REQUIRES A RUBBER BAND TO CINCH THE INCREASINGLY —

SHALL WE SAY "JOLLY" — GIRTH OF OUR INVITATION-PACKED

DATE BOOKS. IF IT'S NOT A FLYER FOR A CHRISTMAS PAGEANT,

IT'S A MEMO REMINDING YOU ABOUT THE HOLIDAY SHINDIG

AT THE OFFICE. ALL OF THIS MERRIMENT IS, OF COURSE,

LOADS OF FUN. BUT IT MAKES SCHEDULING A PARTY AT

THIS TIME OF YEAR A DAUNTING PROSPECT.

I HAVE KNOWN HOSTS AND HOSTESSES who let their innate sense of competition duke this one out for them. They start addressing invitations and humming a medley of "Eye of the Tiger" and "Jingle Bell Rock" even before pumpkins and Halloween costumes hit the stores. But fear not! I am here to say that scheduling a party is a lot like decorating for one: A little innovation goes a long way. Take the party I designed for a couple of New Yorkers with lots of holiday spirit, but not a lot of time to deck-the-halls.

Michael and Angela wanted to enjoy a festive evening at home with friends, neighbors, and co-workers, but they wanted to make it easy for their guests to relax without worrying about after-work trips to the mall or the other obligations of those "jolly" little date books. Even more importantly, they wanted it to capture the youthful sense of play and holiday wonder that trays of cubed cheese and plastic cups of wine never do. This is where I come in.

Instead of the same old cider and appetizers, I designed a sparkling, modern "Crystal Christmas" dessert party that would appeal even to the overbooked. Guests could arrive after stopping in at other parties, or finishing up last-minute shopping, only to find the sweet reward of relaxing with friends. The goal here was to capture the soul of sophistication with elegant details, and the giddiness of every inner-child with an outrageous spread of sweets. Forget visions of sugar plums: Silver trays topped with an exquisite selection of red-and-white cookies, cupcakes, peppermint sticks, and more sat atop modern glass vases stocked with alternating layers of frosty rock candy and robust cranberries. Along with the smart, sleek color scheme — a tribute to that icon of Christmas treats, the candy cane — chic bouquets of amaryllis and calla lilies, extravagant crystal jewel-drops, and a selection of refined holiday cocktails wooed grown-up sensibilities. Whether you crave sweetness or simplicity during the holidays, it's evenings like this one that make the season truly merry.

SCHEDULING A PARTY IS A LOT LIKE DECORATING FOR ONE: A LITTLE INNOVATION GOES A LONG WAY.

# The Look

## A STUDY IN CONTRASTS

Nothing captivates the eye or lightens the heart like the fun-loving play of colors and textures, and that is why contrast, as a design principle, sets the perfect tone for a holiday party that is at once modern and fanciful. Update the old green-and-red Christmas color palette with a bolt from the closet of Saint Nick: Red and white throughout a party space will surround your guests with the chromatic equivalent of cherries and cream. Perch delectable sweets on vases of different heights to lead the eye on an adventurous tour, up and down, and across a dynamic spread of colorful treats. Pair glossy and matte surfaces, like glass ornaments and feathers, for simple and stunning displays. Most important, keep these themes consistent from room to room: Contrast falls into chaos if it isn't rigorously maintained.

In Michael and Angela's apartment, I used the red-and-white color scheme to tie together the whole space, from the sparkling wreath at the front door to the luxurious throw draped over the piano to the enchanting array of desserts in the kitchen. I dressed the tree according to the same simple theme, with candy cane–striped ornaments glimmering all over. Even the

gifts at the base of the tree added to the gleeful design: Red-and-white wrapping paper, featuring a variety of contrasting patterns and textures, combined with different bows and ribbons of the same two colors for a refreshing Yuletide zing. From the twinkling crystal drops that brightly punctuated the entire apartment, to the dazzling cloth of red velvet and white feathers that dressed up the kitchen counter, it was a sight to see. On the traditional Christmas tree, I hung candy ornaments, red lights, feather clusters, and hanging crystals. It looked like a virtual forest of candy canes! And, sure enough, as guests arrived, peeled off a few layers, and surveyed the scene, they did so with the wide eyes of children racing downstairs first thing on Christmas morning.

## SIMPLE DOOR, SPLASHY DECOR:
# Creating a Festive Red and White Wreath

THE MOMENT YOUR GUESTS ARRIVE, whether by driveway or hallway, it's always a good idea to greet them with a splash of decor, hinting at the festivities to come. The perfectly round and cheery wreath serves this purpose wonderfully. Every year I attempt a fresh take on this staple. For this modern party, I clustered red, white, and opal baubles together with a shiny satin bow and a few dangling strands of chandelier crystals. I think of this as the Chanel-necklace-meets-gumball-machine look. Not only does it invoke all of the finest things in life, it also captures the truly exquisite kind of fun that awaits your guests behind the front door.

- Use wire to attach strings of red, white, and opal ornaments to a basic wire wreath structure (available at places like Home Depot or florist shops).

- Attach a pre-tied, red satin bow with a little more wire.

- Hang the wreath with wire wrapped in red ribbon.

- Attach dangling strands of chandelier crystals (which can be purchased at a chandelier parts shop or a lighting store) with — you guessed it — more wire.

# Give the Gift of an Invitation

EVERYONE GETS A THRILL when a party invitation arrives in the mail, especially when it's customized, boxed, and wrapped in ribbon. For this year's holiday party, forgo a mass e-mail and opt for good old-fashioned snail-mail; a little effort at the post office now makes a big statement later. Although Angela and Michael's elegant invitations look as though they were assembled by an ambitious team of Santa's elves, I can assure you that I made them in one afternoon, using Microsoft Word on my home PC. You can do the same.

## HOW TO MAKE PEPPERMINT INVITES

- Print each invitation with red ink on good quality card stock and then glue it to a slightly larger red velvet card. Glue this to an even larger white card.

- Carefully add small red crystals around the perimeter with tiny dabs of glue.

- Package each invitation in a cute red box decorated with a striking, wide red-and-white ribbon.

- Add peppermint candy "buttons" to the ribbon with glue.

# The Scent

## A PRESCRIPTION FOR PEPPERMINT

With all the parties to attend, gifts to wrap, and halls to deck, Christmas is one of those holidays that inspires both giddy excitement and utter exhaustion. That's why the refreshing scent of peppermint puts the perfect finish on this evening affair. Known for its ability to soothe tired caroling voices and promote stress release, just a zing of peppermint in the air has a way of instantly relaxing the mind without putting it to sleep. The trick is to avoid overdoing it, which, in case you're wondering, happens at the moment when your guests start wondering if Altoids has a factory in the neighborhood. At Michael and Angela's sweet soiree, I lit gently scented peppermint-striped candles in a few corners of the apartment — an easy and affordable way to spike the senses without drowning them. As the aromas of freshly baked cookies and mulled winter spices, like cinnamon and cardamom, drifted from room to room, the faintest kiss of peppermint brightened the air, lifting the guests' spirits and voices even higher.

# The Touch

### A TOUCH OF GLASS

The meanings and traditions of Christmas generate so many different feelings in people. Maybe that's why it's so easy to forget that Christmas has a feeling of its own, too. It's the feel of satin ribbons and scratchy pine needles, smooth glass ornaments and nubby woolen stockings, shiny wrapping paper and featherlight tissue paper, and fur and tinsel. Throughout Angela and Michael's party, I paired smooth surfaces of velvet, crystal, glass ornaments, and feathers with the gentle prickly edges of Christmas tree spikes and star fruit slices. I draped feather boa–trimmed velvet over the dining table, piano, and kitchen island to create a soft background for the shiny silver plates and glass vases, and I accented glass bowls with feathers and shimmering ornaments. I extended this combination of textures to the food selection, pairing weightless meringues and peppermint marshmallows with crunchy rock candy and crystal sugar–coated cookies. If anxiously anticipating the mysterious arrival of Saint Nick kept you on your toes as a tot, then this energetic play of contrasts will fill your holiday world, once more, with the excitement of childhood.

## CANDY, COOKIES, AND CHRISTMAS COCKTAILS

Sweet is not the final word when it comes to catering a dessert party. First of all, there are levels of sweetness. There are subtle, cream-based desserts, such as cheesecakes and custard tarts; denser, sugar-based treats, such as candy canes and marshmallows; and, finally, fruity desserts, like dried cranberries and fresh strawberries. Serving a range of desserts can satisfy each of your guests, no matter how sweet their tooth. Secondly, a selection of festive cocktails is essential. In addition to red and white wine, I like to offer bubbly champagne cocktails, spiked hot cider, and a special ice-cold vodka martini at holiday parties. Try coming up with your own signature cocktail or borrow the ones I served at Angela and Michael's party.

## PASSIONATE PINK CHRISTMAS

1 ounce Alizé Red Passion liqueur

Moët and Chandon champagne to fill

Star fruit soaked in pomegranate juice (to color red) for garnish

Pour Alizé liqueur in an old-fashioned champagne glass. Add champagne and garnish with star fruit slice.

## ELFIN MAGIC

5 ounces warm hard apple cider

1 ounce Southern Comfort

Green candy cane for garnish

Pour warm cider into glass mug. Add Southern Comfort and garnish with candy cane. Add a splash of spiced rum (to make a little different).

## SNOWY COSMOPOLITAN

1½ ounces Belvedere Cytrus Vodka

¼ ounce triple sec or Cointreau

¼ ounce white cranberry juice

¼ ounce lime juice

Apple for garnish

Fill a cocktail shaker with ice. Add all ingredients, shake, and strain into martini glass. Garnish with an apple slice cut in the shape of a snowflake.

# The Sound

SLEIGH BELLS AND SANTA CLAUS ROCK

It's crucial to kick off a holiday party with upbeat music. For Angela and Michael's party I expanded the typical holiday repertoire from "Silent Night" and "Jingle Bells" to include more contemporary songs like Eartha Kitt's "Santa Baby" and "Last Christmas" by George Michael and some of my other favorites, listed here:

Christina Aguilera: *My Kind of Christmas*

The Carpenters: *Christmas Portrait*

Jon Bon Jovi: *Please Come Home for Christmas*

Whitney Houston: *The Preacher's Wife* soundtrack

Amy Grant: *Christmas to Remember*

Johnny Mathis: *Merry Christmas*

Barbra Streisand: *Christmas Memories*

This hip, retro approach adds a theatrical, karaoke element to a traditional caroling session. That said, don't leave your tongue-in-cheek all night long; at the end of the day, the season and the bonds between us that it reinforces call for sincerity. That's why I opted for slow, but not somber tunes as Michael and Angela said their good-byes. As usual, Bing Crosby's "White Christmas" really hit the right note.

Needless to say, the candy-striped Christmas gathering swept everyone up in a significantly more jubilant mood than a standard-issue white Christmas-themed one. At the end of the evening, Angela commented that the joyful buzz of laughter and conversation that remained throughout must have been fueled by a long-overdue sugar rush. We were both savoring our very last chocolate truffle (and second-to-last Snowy Cosmo) of the night, so we had to laugh. But the knowing smiles that followed confirmed what we both knew: No amount of sugar can generate the warmth and goodwill that the guests radiated. And, for that matter, no amount of sugar can account for the rousing, if a little experimental, harmonies achieved during an enthusiastic rendition of "Good King Wenceslas." On the other hand, a lively celebration that blends the magic of youth with mature elegance can give the holiday spirit a whole new meaning.

# Tutera Tips

1 Place peppermint candles in the powder room, coat room, and foyer to keep a fresh (and thematic) perfume circulating.

2 Prolong the life of your Christmas tree by adding polyacrylamide gel crystals to the water it sits in.

3 Line velvet tablecloths with feather boas for a chic and truly "Divine" naughty Santa effect. Attach with a needle and thread or with safety pins, but be sure to avoid any kind of pin that can stick out and prick you.

4 According to feng shui, hanging clear quartz crystals can enhance and correct the flow of Chi (energy). Try hanging a crystal in your bedroom window and see if you feel the difference — but remember to keep the crystal clean!

5 Create a candy cane–striped pattern of lights by alternating red votives with crystal-trimmed white votive holders along your mantel or piano.

6 Create cocktail garnishes in the shape of snowflakes by using cookie cutters and round slices of apples.

7 I take great inspiration from my friends over at Cartier who wrap the entire historic flagship building with an enormous red ribbon every December. Try "wrapping" your own house . . . but start small. For example, I wrapped red satin ribbons around square light fixtures and hung them in Angela and Michael's kitchen. You can also tie ribbons around square vases or containers.

8 Spill rock candy (available in bulk at candy shops or online) onto a silver tray. This simple flourish instantly re-creates the glamorous effect of piles of uncut (and edible) diamonds.

9 Place a bouquet of elegant white lilies on a piano, broad windowsill, or foyer table for a striking look. Just remember: For this party, it's all about contrast!

10 Print the lyrics to your favorite Christmas songs and have them handy. With a party this delightful, you never know when your guests might feel the need to burst into song.

## GREAT FORTUNE AND GOOD LUCK: A CHINESE NEW YEAR PARTY

*for sixteen*

## February feels like a transitional month

FOR MOST PEOPLE. WITH CHRISTMAS, HANUKAH, AND NEW
YEAR'S WRAPPED UP, WE TEND TO HUNKER DOWN FOR THE
END OF THE WINTER WITH NOTHING MORE THAN THE HOPE
THAT SPRINGTIME WILL DELIVER US TO DAFFODILS AND
BUTTERFLIES SOMETIME SOON. YVE AND ZANE ARPEL,
TWO OF MY DEAREST FRIENDS FROM WAY BACK,
FIND THIS RESIGNATION TOTALLY UNACCEPTABLE.

INSTEAD, THEY PREFER TO SPEND Boston's bleakest winter month in the rapturous warmth of the two-week-long ceremonies and celebrations for the Chinese New Year. Every February, they bundle up like Polartec snowmen and head to Chinatown, where the Lantern Festival that marks the end of the holiday floods the streets with a parade of brightly burning lanterns, colorful decorations, and fireworks displays. This year, however, they decided to bring the happy occasion of a Chinese New Year to *their* house — where it's a little warmer — and they asked yours truly to make it happen.

I absolutely *loved* the idea of shaking up the plodding mood of late winter by celebrating a different kind of holiday — and I, myself, love Chinese New Year. What could be better than a holiday honoring luck, loved ones, and abundance for the upcoming year, replete with ornate dragon kites, drums, and delectable culinary treats? It's like Thanksgiving and the Fourth of July mashed together in the most beautiful way: A tribute to family, food, and good tidings with some nifty pyrotechnics thrown in. But I knew I would have to take it even further for Yve and Zane, not only because they are the only friends I have who don't get offended when I affectionately call them Evil and Zaney — but because when it comes to holiday celebrations, they think so far outside the box they don't even know it exists. For two preppy New Englanders, they really know how to loosen their canvas whale belts and dream up the most fantastical party scenes ever, whether or not it's possible to actually make those dreams a reality. Let me give you an example: They wanted me to transform their three-car garage into a crimson Chinatown outpost for sixteen dinner guests.

I've turned a San Diego hangar into a French château, a Texas hotel ballroom into a Russian tearoom, and a posh Connecticut estate into Amsterdam's Red-Light District. So I told them, "No way," but instead, I wowed them by outfitting their heated three-car garage, a valuable area so often forgotten by hosts short on space, in the emperor's most fabulous new clothes. Of course, these clothes came with a little reinterpretation, and this is one of the great things about celebrating a holiday that is new to your family: You can go traditional or you can adapt it to your vision, ready-to-wear or couture. For instance, I knew that part of what Yve and

Zane loved about celebrating the Chinese New Year in the lively streets of Boston's Chinatown was the intoxicating mix of all of the various cultures that came together. So, instead of carefully re-creating every official rite of the holiday, I made their party reflect that same glorious melting pot. The results were stunning, but simple. With bamboo floor mats to cover the concrete, some candles and pillows, a few bolts of red satiny fabric and Chinese silk, and an inspired Asian-fusion menu, the fireworks were entirely figurative.

## BLUSHING RED, PINK, AND ORANGE

If one of the fundamental charms of a holiday is the way it can make one day seem utterly out of the ordinary, then one of the greatest holiday charms of this party is the amazing sense of warmth it generates in such frigid times. Surely the spirits rise with the coming of the New Year itself, but it is the decor of the party — more than the furnace or even the occasion — that expresses the positive energy and heat that will thaw out your guests.

This party all began with the high temperature of the color scheme, which I took directly from some of my favorite lanterns that were in the Lantern Festival. I enveloped the entire space, including the tent-style cloth that covered the ceiling, in deep tones of crimson, fuchsia, and pale orange. The warmth and consistency of these tones surrounded guests in a truly happy color palette and, from the tablecloth to the napkins, made guests feel comfortable in what could have otherwise been a drafty and cavernous space. Never underestimate the power of color to create a mood or a feeling. It's one of my favorite tricks.

Of course, the flickering light cast by clusters of red pillar candles of various heights also contributed to the festive glow of the evening. As their candlelight combined with that of the orange Chinese lanterns scattered about the corners of the room and hanging from the ceiling, guests wondered at the strange and alluring shadows they cast. As glamorous and hypnotic as all of these innovative lighting designs are, however, it's important to remain practical, too. That's why I strategically positioned pebble-coated votives all over the surface of the table to illuminate the space between dishes. Not only did they draw out the dramatic lines of the place settings, but they also guarded against accidental spills that might have disturbed the scene.

Most important of all, however, the minimalist lines and soft colors of the floral arrangement brought a vital serenity to the bold and romantic

elements of the holiday decor; the evening should feel warm and exceptional, not oppressive in its uniform intensity. For the table runner, I assembled pale green moss, dried and fresh bamboo, and a variety of orchids in a low-lying arrangement that took up a limited amount of table space. The result was like a peaceful garden spanning the length of the table. A bamboo chandelier, made from four pieces of bamboo wired together and accented with orchids and smilax vine, brought the details of the table to a higher level. These delicate details not only united what I think are some of the most simple, beautiful, and symbolic elements of Pan-Asian floral design (bamboo is for luck), they allowed me to satisfy what has become an absolute *passion* for orchids.

A few years ago, when I designed the Cancer Research Foundation fundraiser in Washington, D.C., for fifteen hundred people, the ambassador of Singapore marveled at all the hundreds of orchids I brought in, commenting that she felt transported back home. You can imagine my delight! Now, whenever I can, I go nuts with a truckload of delicate orchids and I'm as happy as can be. If you have a passion for another kind of flower, take advantage of the freedom you have in establishing a new tradition of holiday celebration, and use it to bring warmth to *your* Chinese New Year. Just make sure that it offers either an innovative counterpoint to the decor as a whole or a quiet continuity to it.

The final visual detail that brought all these elements from the East and West into harmony was the unusual take on a typical place setting. Here are a few fun tips to get you from china to China:

- In a playful nod to your chic take-out meal, serve the first course in a cute, bright red Chinese take-out box.

- Set geometric plates, an assortment of minimalist glassware, and bamboo-style flatware on an angle to create clean, simple lines.

- Pick luxe materials that draw from traditional elements of Chinese design like lacquer and gilt, and make sure they maintain the warm, rich color scheme of the room. Here, I used glazed black plates and gold-plated flatware.

- Offer black lacquer chopsticks for your more agile guests. In the arrangement I use, they not only present an appropriately stylish alternative to Western traditions of dining, they accent the finish of the plates.

- Pluck a color from the larger color scheme and use it somewhere in the setting to unify all elements. The double-rolled pink napkin that sits with two orchid heads in the center of this particular setting brings a much-needed splash of color into the mix. And even better, the gold-flecked paper napkin ring that bundles it together refers to both the invitation that guests received and the earthly art of the Asian floral design throughout the room.

- Tickle the curiosity of your guests with a chic dinner menu. For Yve and Zane's party, I simply downloaded the Chinese character for "dinner" from the Internet and printed it, along with the various courses of the evening, on sleek, red vellum paper.

- Provide guests with a traditional tea glass to accompany their dessert course. The pale green ones I used added a cool counterpoint to the prevalent tones of red and pink.

There is no wisdom greater than kindne

### ORANGE BLOSSOMS BLOOMING

Unless you're stuck in rush-hour traffic in New York City's Chinatown, the scents and perfumes sold there are most often simple, clean, calming, and subtle. Think jasmine, ginger, and citrus, and before you fall into a restful state of aromatherapy bliss, don't forget to bring these scents into your entertaining space. Especially if it otherwise serves as a garage! I firmly believe these restful scents did half the work of transforming the feel of Yve and Zane's space, and whether you want to use a basement, living room, or your regular dining room to bring this party into your own life, they can do the same for yours. They are freshness incarnate, and it is perhaps for this reason that they have been so essential to the celebration of a new start at Chinese New Year.

Traditionally, Chinese families decorate their living rooms with vases of fragrant blossoms and platters of oranges, tangerines, and candy before the big day. I put a spin on this tradition by using orange blossom water to freshen the bathrooms and the foyer, and sprinkling some on the concrete floor before laying down the bamboo mats where guests would later sit. Heaven!

# The Touch

## SATIN ROBES AND SILK SLIPPERS

I wanted Yve and Zane's guests to arrive at this party and suddenly feel transported — as if by time machine — to the luxurious inner sanctum of a great Chinese emperor. So, while the red and orange visuals worked their magic on the eyes, the textures of silk and satin cushions and smooth bamboo mats worked its magic on the feet. Yve and Zane offered guests the option to remove their winter shoes and go sock-footed, or slip into some velvet Chinese slippers provided at the front door. By the time guests were seated, the seduction had already begun . . . once they began to lounge as only emperors do, they were officially in another world.

## HOW TO
# Lower the Table

ONE OF THE MORE CLEVER elements of this rein-vented space is the low table and surrounding cushions. It's very Asian, relaxing, and it's not hard to create. You can use any rectangular table that has folding legs.

- Tuck the legs under and then place at least two sturdy crates or supports (with a height of about 12 to 18 inches) beneath it. The key is that the supports are exactly the same height and wide enough to support the tabletop without letting it tilt even the slightest. We used six large crates filled with bricks.

- Surround the table with large flat sofa cushions. If you have patio furniture with waterproof cushion pads, use them.

- Place the cushions around the table to form a soft, seamless "bench."

- Then, cover them with heavy fabric, decorative rugs, or with a lighter fabric.

- Cover the table with a colorful fabric, preferably red-, fuchsia-, or orange-colored, and then accent with a chic silk or satin runner.

- Finally, toss extra cushions onto the "benches" to make the setting even cozier.

# The Taste

## PAN-ASIAN PERFECTION

Cooking dishes that come from the cuisine of another culture can be a daunting affair, especially when you're doing it for company. In fact, the mere prospect intimidates a lot of amateur chefs who would otherwise love to celebrate foreign flavors and occasions. But who says ordering Chinese should be reserved for overworked Wall Street bachelors and under-worked couch potatoes? If you want to bring authentic flavors to the scene of a party, nothing beats it. Of course, when I choose to order-in for an elaborate holiday dinner party, I don't reach for the menu flapping in the mailbox; I go highbrow. Yve and Zane directed me to their favorite Asian-fusion restaurant, and I worked with the chef and staff to come up with a great menu.

It all began with the mellow bite of a green tea martini made for the occasion. I wanted to introduce guests right away to the play of counter-pointed flavors and textures that is central to most Asian cuisines. The zing of the ginger and vodka mixed against the delicate tannins of the tea perfectly expressed the invigorating spark of this cozy gathering, but also the sweet-spicy-sour sensations of the menu to follow. For the first course, guests dined on a bracing rendition of lemon-pepper shrimp and crispy crab wontons served with a sweet plum sauce. Next, they set their sights and their chopsticks on the sweet acidity of mango chicken and the creamy richness of coconut rice, a Thai inspiration. The final course reintroduced these sweet notes of coconut milk in an entirely new way as a smooth ice-cream accompaniment to a hot and crispy banana spring roll. Together, the flavors were homey but nimble, fresh, and

## A Chinese New Year Menu

LEMON-PEPPER SHRIMP WITH CHIVES AND SPROUTS

CRAB WONTONS WITH PLUM SAUCE

MANGO CHICKEN WITH COCONUT RICE

BANANA SPRING ROLLS WITH COCONUT ICE CREAM

SELECTION OF HERBAL TEAS

exciting, too; exactly what Yve and Zane had in mind for their newest holiday gathering. It might have been unconventional, but just as it always has in Chinese households, the tremendous amount of food served as a delicious symbol of abundance and wealth for all.

## GREEN TEA MARTINI

3 ounces Belvedere Vodka
1 ounce green tea
Splash of ginger liqueur

Shake with ice, strain, pour into a martini glass, and accent with an orchid head.

# The Sound

## GENTLE CHIMES IN THE WIND

While the sounds of cars zooming through Chinatown are certainly stimulating, we opted for the soundtrack of another side of China: the one that is filled with gardens, rivers, and gentle chimes. I hung wood chimes along the driveway and then placed one more in the entrance to the dining area. Remember, a little chime can go a long way, so be sparing with these sound effects: You want to achieve a graceful tinkling of sounds, rather than a chorus of clangs. To foreground the distant chimes, I played a selection of soothing ambient music that had some echoes of traditional Chinese melodies like these CDs:

Enya: *A Day Without Rain*

Karunesh: *Nirvana Café*

Zingaia: *Dancers of Twilight Buddha-Bar,* Vol. VI

Steven Halpern: *Music for Sound Healing*

When this party was still in its earliest planning stages — when the garage was still the garage and not a portal to another world — celebrating the Chinese New Year seemed like a singular event. But by the time guests finished their final cups of tea and slipped back into their shoes to leave — as if slipping back into the outside world itself — I couldn't help but feel touched by the anticipation with which people were already talking about "this time next year." What began as an innovative expression of warmth, cheer, and togetherness had become something more; it had become a tradition. Sure enough, the message attached to the gold fortune cookie Yve and Zane gave me as a party favor foretold it all: "You will find happiness for many years to come." Now I know at least one time and one place where that will always be true, whether it is the year of the horse, monkey, dog, or rat.

# Tutera Tips

1 For a striking Chinese New Year's invitation, go for gold. Start with a red, square "self-mailer" envelope and attach layers of alternating gold and red papers. Top the layered paper with a square sheet of gold vellum printed with the party information.

2 Cut and paste Chinese symbols — easily found on the Web — to your printed materials (invitations, menu cards, etc). Try using the Chinese symbols for the words "invitation" and "menu."

3 Spray paint plain white paper lanterns for a custom look. (Always spray outside or in a well-ventilated area.)

4 Traditional Chinese etiquette dictates that you must bring a bag of oranges and tangerines when visiting family or friends anytime during the two-week-long Chinese New Year celebration. So, offer tangerines and oranges as gifts to your guests or to your host(s).

5 Allow your guests to remove their shoes when you've got a cushioned seating arrangement. While you're at it, leave a few extra-strength jasmine candles burning near the shoe depot.

6 Create a draw to the party: Hang lanterns and chimes from the trees along the walkway to the front door.

7 Create a delicate napkin ring out of ornamental grasses: Wrap a strip of vellum around a rolled napkin. Then, punch three holes in the vellum. Using ornamental grass, tie the two sides together with a crisscross design. Accent with two orchid heads.

8 Orchids, although pricey, are a hardy and strong flower. Use potted orchids as decor and you will enjoy them for years to come!

9 When having a party with seating on the floor, remember that the ceiling will need to have decor added, too. It's about having balance — a little yin and yang.

10 If you use plastic Chinese take-out containers (like the red ones we used), you can wash and reuse them for your next party — a very clever and cost-effective idea.

4

## SPECIAL OCCASIONS AND MILESTONE CELEBRATIONS

GLIMPSE INTO THE FUTURE:
A WEDDING PROPOSAL DINNER CELEBRATION

FOR THE KIDS: A PLAYFUL BIRTHDAY PARTY

LOVE GROWS IN THE FOREST: AN ANNIVERSARY PARTY

ometimes life seems to pass in a glorious blur. Faces and moments fly by at top speed as we grow up, get smart, and move from one challenge to the next. With the alluring mystery of the future laid out before us, how could we do anything else but race ahead to reinvent its possibilities and, in the process, ourselves? It's part of our culture — just ask Madonna. Here's the rub, though: Life is more than a series of wardrobe changes and, unlike Madonna, the undisputed Goddess of Reinvention, few of us have an entire industry to record the changes we undergo throughout the course of life. That's why it's so important to stop and really savor all the milestones — all those accomplishments, personal or professional — that help us become who we're going to be. And, short of a thrilling world tour, the right kind of party can transform the speed of life into a meaningful appreciation of accomplishment, a delicious memory of what's important, and a truly pleasurable experience shared with those who matter most.

Perhaps the best thing of all about milestone celebrations is that anybody can decide when one is necessary, whether it's a wedding anniversary, twenty-five years in business, a big victory at work, a school graduation, the completion of a marathon, victory in a personal battle, or a simple birthday. Over time, milestones add up. Each new celebration rep-

resents a significant point in an individual's development. For this reason, the most important aspect to remember about planning such an occasion is to place the honoree(s) in the foreground. I cannot stress this point enough. Unlike a straightforward dinner party or a holiday, which privileges the event itself, milestone celebrations are tributes to people and their lives. So, no matter how eccentric your Great-Aunt Maude may be, when you celebrate her sixtieth birthday, she should feel like an absolute *star* for being exactly who she is. They don't call them celebrities for nothing; milestone parties are the rare occasions when all of us ordinary citizens join the ranks of the lavishly celebrated.

In practical terms, however, focusing on the personality and accomplishment of the honoree plays out a little differently than it does in Hollywood. There will be no tearful recollections of childhood printed in *People*. Instead, the idea is to plan the details of the festivities — from the menu to the decor to the music — in such a way that his or her experience of the occasion is filled with significance. Because every sense should act as a reminder of what's being celebrated, it is especially important to honor all the five senses in entertaining at these events. Picking a location that means something is an important first step. For instance, the intimate proposal dinner that I describe in the following chapter takes place on a floating dock in the middle of a lake — an original, wordless tribute to the couple's summertime courtship there years before. With being surrounded by all the romantic natural elements, remember to entice all five senses for this special dinner for two. Better still, the meaning of a location can be made even more tangible if it's decorated with mementos related to the milestone, whether they're photographs, dried flowers, or a newly abandoned office chair that reminds everyone of the liberation at hand.

THE RIGHT KIND OF PARTY CAN TRANSFORM THE SPEED OF LIFE INTO A MEANINGFUL APPRECIATION OF ACCOMPLISHMENT.

A careful selection of music is also an essential element of the honoree's big night. For an anniversary party, contact the couple's lifelong friends to find out not only "their" song, but also all the songs they've danced to over the years. Trust me, when they do the Hustle to their favorite disco classic and remember that time in their lives together, it won't be the complicated footwork that makes their hearts race. Last, but not least, the menu is another great place to incorporate a special detail, whether it references the past or the future now possible. If a colleague you've worked with every day for thirty years retires to live at the beach, why not give them a taste of the good life to come with flavors fresh from the ocean? Stars can be demanding, it's true, but whether the honoree dreams in formal attire or flip-flops, combining that dream with the meaning of the occasion in sensual form is the top priority.

The other crucial element of a fantastic milestone celebration involves the guests. Most parties draw a few casual acquaintances that drop in to say hello or to mingle before another event. But you will find very few guests at a golden anniversary who are there for the open bar; these guests come because they care. A great way to deepen and reward that expression of warmth is to design the invitation as a keepsake by packaging it in a silk box. So many people like to commemorate a special day by saving an important invitation but have nowhere to store or display it. By incorporating the display into the invitation itself, every guest can own a reminder of the event without lifting a finger.

Another great way to acknowledge the importance of the guests at a milestone celebration is to create an environment that allows friends and family to really *experience* the meaning of the day alongside the honoree. Many of the sensual cues that speak to the honoree will also speak to the other guests, but sometimes I like to take things a step further. For example, in the following pages I describe a twenty-fifth anniversary party set in a winding, wooded landscape behind the country home of the lucky couple. As guests followed glowing candelabras from one clearing to the next for different stages of the party, they experienced the sensation of being on a magical journey improved by the company of loved ones, which was the very kind of journey they had gathered to honor. But you don't need a wooded grove to generate an enthusiastic response to the moment in your crowd; any element of surprise creates an amazing sense of shared experience that makes savoring the occasion a matter of intuition for everyone.

Apart from these two fundamental principles, an unforgettable milestone celebration depends only on a measure of simplicity. Because these parties often draw friends and family of all ages and sensibilities, it's vital to make sure that picky eaters won't go hungry. If the star of the event needs sushi like J. Lo needs Egyptian cotton sheets, find a way to supplement such extravagant touches with plenty of choices for the tempura set, and also for the vegetarians. Likewise, hiring a photographer to immortalize the big night will not only free up your cousin to enjoy the festivities, it will give everyone present the priceless experience of complaining about the paparazzi. Above all else, though, a little simplicity goes a long way if *you* happen to be the host of your own celebration, a circumstance I encourage everyone to embrace. Life is too quick and too fabulous to let it slip by without raising a glass. So, take the time to stop and stare at the beautiful simplicity of the stars above (and life itself!). My only hope is that the tips and ideas that follow will help you shine just as brightly as those diamonds in the sky.

## GLIMPSE INTO THE FUTURE: A WEDDING PROPOSAL DINNER CELEBRATION

for two

As far as I'm concerned, the real moment of

TRUTH  AT MOST SPORTS EVENTS DOES NOT COME WHEN THE

BEST TEAM WINS OR LOSES; IT COMES WITH THE JUMBOTRON

PROPOSAL. THE INSTANT A NERVOUS SUITOR ASKS FOR HIS

GIRLFRIEND'S HAND IN MARRIAGE ON THAT GIANT COLOR

SCREEN, YOU CAN TELL WHETHER IT'S HER ULTIMATE FANTASY

OR HER WORST NIGHTMARE, NO MATTER WHAT SHE ANSWERS.

UNFORTUNATELY, FOR MANY WOMEN (THOUGH CERTAINLY

NOT ALL — GO TEAM!) IT'S THE LATTER.

EVEN THE MOST CAPABLE and sensitive of men can lose their minds a little bit when planning such a pivotal moment, forgetting altogether the most important rule of all for marriage proposals: If you're going to share a life together then *both* of you should be reflected in the moment that this life begins. So, when a gentleman called to see if I would help him set an unforgettable scene for a proposal to his childhood sweetheart, I was happy to help. Every time I stop an unwanted Jumbotron spectacle I know I'm on Earth for a reason.

Once I met Thom Bowman, though, I knew that no man in a seer-sucker suit would propose amidst the scent of stale beer and crushed peanut shells. He simply knew the occasion meant everything to his girl-friend, Sally, and needed some help bringing her wildest dream of that moment to the life they shared. I was on board. He began with the specifics: Sally had been perusing bridal magazines since she was ten years old, so in yardage, we were talking the whole nine. But she wasn't afraid of a little slapstick either — she's a big fan of romantic comedies from the forties — so it had to be quirky and unexpected; he wanted to hear her gasp with surprise and the laugh he loved. Beyond that, he knew only that the big moment had to take place on the lake behind their house. During the humid, lazy summers of their teen years, they'd fallen for each other on long days by that lake.

For brides-to-be who dream of this occasion as long as Sally has, I feel it's important to bring the feeling of an actual wedding to the space of the proposal. Because the couple should feel the full significance of the amaz-ing moment that lies ahead, I wanted to create a series of sensations that would fill Thom and Sally with anticipation for the future. I had to build an experience of wonder and surprise to honor such a special moment. But the combination of slapstick and silk didn't really fall into place until I saw the lone floating dock in the middle of their lake. Then the real planning began.

At dusk, Thom would lead Sally out to their rowboat for a glide through the water, only to arrive at the floating dock. But the dock would be radically transformed: Chairs outfitted in the finery of a bride and groom would wait at a table for two and classic stripes of black and white and bursts of sparkling crystal would add a touch of 'forties hauteur to the settings. The finest china and crystal would frame a romantic repast and flickering candles and pale blue flowers would complete the scene, along with chilled champagne and a waiting ring. I joked with Thom that the pond was just one soft push away if she turned him down, but somehow I didn't need a crystal ball (or a Jumbotron) to see how this particular fairy tale would end.

# The Look

When I met Thom to plan his extravagant proposal, I asked him to bring a few pictures of Sally so I could get a sense of what she was like. He handed me a small stack of snapshots . . . right away I loved this girl. She had a swaying coiffed bob, a clear affection for her simple pearl necklace, and a knack for fitted suits with pencil skirts. She appeared entirely "put together" though, somehow, I couldn't imagine her spending so much as five minutes agonizing with curlers, makeup, or fancy manicures. She struck me as a twenty-first-century Katharine Hepburn. With that stunner in mind, I began to recall the vivacious humor and romantic spirit of *The Philadelphia Story* when an image came to me.

I had already planned a visual teaser for the big day with chairs "dressed" as bride and groom, champagne on ice, a bride's bouquet of crystal-studded ivory roses, and a special miniature wedding cake, but now a bigger picture was forming. Fun, carefree, and elegant, everything would be decorated with the flair and style of a Hollywood movie set in the forties: bold color contrasts and lots of silver for a sparkly effect. Starting with black-and-white tiles to cover the worn and wet wood of the dock, I worked my way up to a chic black tablecloth with striped black-and-white satin trim, black-and-white silk napkins clasped with rhinestone bracelets, and black-and-white chandelier lampshades perched atop tall tapered candles. I set the table with Sally's dream wedding china and stemware — no less than Waterford and Wedgwood — and draped crystals from the chandelier all over. The only touch of color came from the pastel blue hydrangeas I used to accent the napkins and fill a set of antique silver boxes, as placed at the base of the candelabra.

Now, putting all this together on a small dock wasn't easy — let's just say there were a few stray hydrangea blooms floating around the lake — but it was well worth the effort. Boarding that rowboat at dusk, Sally could never expect to stumble across a fantasy vision like this one. A rickety pond-water proposal? Maybe. But satin and stripes? Even the wily Katharine Hepburn wouldn't see that one coming.

# The Scent

## GARDENIAS ARE FOR LOVERS

The white gardenia with its dark, glossy green leaves has long been a beloved floral accessory for young ladies. Edith Warton envisioned her blushing girls pinning single gardenias to their gowns and her elegant suitors displaying them in buttonholes. By the 1950s (thanks in no small part to Edith), gardenias were ubiquitous on the prom circuit. Today, I love to take this sensual, powerfully fragrant blossom beyond the same old hair clip or corsage. Whenever the right formal, feminine occasion presents itself, I float the blossoms in a shallow glass vase or use them to fill small baskets or velvet pouches. A few strategically placed gardenias can perfume an entire room, but outside the effect is even more stunning when gentle breezes carry its scent of a warm summer garden through the air. For Thom and Sally's tête-a-tête, I placed gardenias in antique silver boxes around the base of the chandelier, letting the sweet aroma waft over the pond and swirl about the dining table. With this one romantic detail in place, no elaborate pyrotechnics would be necessary to produce an evening of unforgettable fireworks.

# The Touch

## A TOUCH OF ROMANCE

Even the most lavish and enthusiastic proposal can create a sense of limbo for the bride-and groom-to-be. I see it all the time. The restaurant is divine, her favorite song is playing, and his favorite scotch is waiting. The ring is perfect and mom — you can imagine her giddy face — is just a cell-phone call away. But there's something about the actual *idea* of a wedding that remains elusive. It's as if they've closed the door to one life but the door to their new life has not yet opened. While I think the engagement provides a crucial "transition" phase (not to mention ample time to plan a great party), I do think there are ways to crack open that door-to-the-future just a little . . . to give the couple a glimpse of the magic and wonder of a real wedding-in-the-making.

Now, I am no scientist; I own no lab coat (unless you count the one I lost in the streets of Paris one Halloween, which we won't get into). After years of working with people to make special occasions touch something deep in their hearts, though, I know for a fact that we all learn best through tangible sensations. So many women tell me that they didn't really "get it" until they slipped into their wedding gown. With this purpose in mind, I built Thom and Sally's proposal dinner around material hints at all the good things to come. The moment Sally sat down in her chair she learned exactly what it meant to be a bride. Covered in a light organza, this chair not only looked the part, it gave the crucial sensation of gown material against Sally's skin — instant gratification! Weddings are for two, though, so Thom also got to experience a little time-travel while sitting against a tux-in-waiting. In fact, the satin tablecloth, silk napkins, and crystal glasses all combined into a kind of tactile foreshadowing of the sensational event to come; a true brush with greatness.

## NO ORDINARY AFFAIR

The main course of Thom and Sally's menu was already set: carats. As for all proposal dinners, assembling the meal itself was simply a matter of picking a supporting cast to play up that sparkling star. If a couple likes to cook together or has shared one incredibly special meal that could be re-created, I always let the meaning of their experience together come through in the dinner itself. But, in general, such a momentous evening deserves sophisticated sensations, the kinds that know better than to impose on a private engagement. This is not *just* a matter of taste; nobody wants to remember the "warmth" of his or her companion's heartburn for eternity.

In this spirit, I designed a meal for Thom and Sally that would be light enough to keep spirits high yet understated enough to leave the star on center stage and lovely enough for the truest love. It all began with thin slices of cold-smoked salmon served on potato pancakes and crepes with crème fraîche. Next, the soft, mild sweetness of plump, steamed lobster tails balanced out the spicy slices of braised fennel that sat by its side. A heart of romaine lettuce holding unadorned kernels of gently roasted sweet corn brought a seasonal note to the dish along with one of springtime's daintiest (and most rare!) offerings, a few sautéed fiddlehead ferns. For the finale, a splendidly simple dish of fresh strawberries and sabayan whipped cream gave Sally and Thom a chance to enjoy their just desserts together.

The beauty of this meal for a romantic dinner, whether or not you're planning to pop the question lies in its unfussy glamour. It's diva flavor with church-girl manners and, despite its ease to prepare, it never fails to impress. And the best part of all? It travels wonderfully in a rowboat.

# The Sound

FLYING FISH AND FOND MEMORIES

If you've ever sat by a lake in the early evening and just listened, you may recall that the volume of the surrounding forest life seems to go up as the sun goes down. There are fish jumping, deer being fleet of foot, frogs croaking and the odd owl cooing itself awake. In all, this makes for a playful soundtrack of creatures leaping and pecking, splashing and darting. It's a magical phonic backdrop for any romantic moment; a mischievous crinkle and crunch to sharpen the senses. I let Sally and Thom enjoy this mischief as they rowed out to their hidden picnic dinner, but once the proposal and gasps and tears had played out, I made sure to have some backup music for the celebratory dinner. Aside from some universally lovable love songs and cute reminders of the occasion (such as ABBA's "I Do, I Do, I Do, I Do, I Do"), I suggested that Thom bring along a selection of songs he and Sally have loved and enjoyed over the years. A proposal dinner is a great time to get thinking about *the* wedding song. The couple can reminisce about tapes they sang along to on long road trips or a song they still always play on Sunday mornings. The process of picking just one song often means reeling through dozens of romantic moments. So, when Thom cued up the boom box that I secured in the rowboat, the two of them were able to enjoy a flutter down memory lane as they looked towards the future. Here are some romantic musical suggestions:

Frank Sinatra: *Duets*, Vols. 1 and 2

Cyndi Lauper: *At Last*

Joss Stone: *The Soul Sessions*, "I've Fallen in Love With You"

Elvis: *The 50 Greatest Love Songs*, "Can't Help Falling in Love"

Aretha Franklin: *30 Greatest Hits*, "Baby I Love You"

Dinah Washington: *Golden Classics,* "What a Diff'rence a Day Made"

ABBA: *Very Best of ABBA,* "I Do, I Do, I Do, I Do, I Do"

Faith Hill: *Breathe,* title song

Alicia Keys: *Diary of Alicia Keys,* "If I Ain't Got You"

I'll never forget how Sally's splash into the water echoed all the way to the house. . . . No, not really. In fact, as the evening light started to fade I would have happily received any sign of Sally's response. Sitting back at the house, munching on the extra strawberries, I waited with Sally's family for the verdict to come in. As would be expected of a gentleman of his character, Thom had asked for Sally's hand in advance. As far as I could tell, these two were perfect for each other. I knew she would say yes. My only anxiety revolved around the volume and timing of a frog croaking nearby. But my fear was put to rest a few hours later when two enormous smiles eased toward the shore and I felt the deepest happiness in return. I didn't ask the two of them any questions, so my story of that evening ends here; it's theirs now.

# Tutera Tips

1 When planning to surprise your intended, pick a one-of-a-kind location, but make sure it is safe. If you use a dock, check its stability and attach a long rope to a secure area on land.

2 When using black and white for decor, always use a touch of another color to soften the boldness. My personal favorite is periwinkle blue.

3 Save the decorated chairs — they will look amazing at the wedding.

4 Use the theme of your proposal evening to inspire the design for your wedding and honeymoon. Along every step of the way, you can share the happiness of that first special night with your guests and, by the end of the whole event, each moment will resonate in unison with it.

5 The "rhinestone" napkin holders are so easy to make! Just purchase some inexpensive costume jewelry on a strand and tie it around the napkins.

6 Don't fret about the shortage of electrical sockets in natural settings. Take the opportunity to set a romantic mood with candelabras and beautiful vintage lampshades.

7 Add crystals for an additional sparkle to the bride's bouquet and groom's boutonniere.

8 Nothing kills a mood like gazing deeply into the eyes of . . . a camera. To capture the moment, hire a photographer to take candid photos only for one short portion of the evening.

9 When preparing lobster, always break the tail away from the body. If it hasn't been split, just break off the little flaps and push through to get the meat out in one piece. To avoid any and all shellfish catapults (a real mood killer), serve the lobster tail without its shell. Then it's just a matter of knife and fork.

10 The most romantic desserts are the ones you can enjoy together. Instead of individual slices of cake, for example, leave open the possibility for closer contact. Dipping strawberries in lightly sweet sabayon cream is not only fun and slightly mischievous, it encourages sharing. . . .

## FOR THE KIDS:
## A PLAYFUL
## BIRTHDAY PARTY
*for eight*

When you're growing up, some things take

YEARS TO LEARN: ALGEBRA, RESPONSIBLE CITIZENSHIP, THE

MEANING OF FAMILY, AND THE NAME OF A GOOD THERAPIST.

LUCKILY, SOME THINGS JUST COME NATURALLY, THOUGH, AND

EMBRACING THE THRILL OF A GOOD PARTY IS DEFINITELY AT THE

TOP OF THE LIST, RIGHT AFTER BLINKING. CHILDREN HAVE AN

INNATE COMMITMENT TO THE FREEDOM AND IMAGINATION OF

REVELRY, AND THAT'S WHY I'M A FIRM BELIEVER IN THROWING

THE MOST FANTASTIC PARTIES POSSIBLE FOR THEM.

GREAT LOVERS OF THEATER deserve the finest drama; the most committed sports fans deserve a team that plays with heart and passion; surely connoisseurs of play also deserve seriously great parties. No one should have to face adulthood without at least one truly magical day to remember.

Once *in* adulthood, however, throwing an elaborate party for a band of wild children might seem foolhardy. In their uncontainable glee, little ones have been known to affect the kind of property damage more often associated with rioting mobs, plate tectonics, and the Doppler radar. Things get messy and break. But before you resign yourself to sending your own little tornado to his or her fifteenth helping of cardboard pizza and stale cake at the local roller rink this year, consider the fanciful and fool-proof birthday party I planned to celebrate Phoebe Mills's fifth year.

Phoebe's mother called me with all of the usual concerns that parents have about children's parties. She wanted to go all out but was nervous about throwing the party in her large backyard, which also includes an original one-room schoolhouse that she'd just finished renovating. How would she keep the kids from romping off into parts of the yard that she couldn't supervise? Was it possible to plan a party that looked like a kid's fantasy but was also low-maintenance? In my best imitation of Obi-Wan Kenobi, I smiled knowingly. But without the robes, the sandals, and the glowing aura, I knew I'd have to do a little more explaining, so I sketched out the basics right then and there.

All great children's parties should rely on a few very basic essentials: bright colors, group activities, and, perhaps most crucial of all, safe and durable materials, like plastic and rubber. The trick is to create a complete, focused environment that captures the children — I mean that in both the whimsical and literal way. For Phoebe's party, oversized paddle balloons of pink, purple, and orange would be scattered over the yard around the party table and staked in place, creating a goofy but effective boundary for the action. The schoolhouse would be filled with floating, beribboned balloons in a variety of polka-dotted colors, gifts would be gathered on the old-fashioned desks, and easels and finger paints would await all budding artists. At the center of the yard would sit a child-sized table decked in bright pink flowers, wooden blocks, and colorful, unbreakable tableware for a spirited little feast befitting the young and the restless. Whether you use a few of these ideas or all of them or whether you're celebrating the birthday of a child or a child at heart, the eyes will be wide, the smiles big, and the headaches absent.

# The Look

## PLAYTIME COMES TO LIFE

If there's one thing kid's have a knack for, it's blurring the boundary between reality and fantasy. Plastic horses become friends, curtains become ghosts, and teddy bears become the soldiers who protect them. Kids know something about inanimate objects we grown-ups have long since forgotten. With this in mind and my own magical Mary Poppins bag of party tricks at hand, I made it my goal to bring the decor for this birthday party to wild, unbridled life. The entire look of the party began with the invitation. A plastic toy clock in primary colors arrived at guests' homes bearing all the pertinent information and a plucky message every kid loves to hear: "Time for a party."

This surreal interpretation of an everyday object served as a fitting introduction to the environment I built around the idea of a child's fantastical vision of the world. Carousel horses rose on posts around the garden so that they seemed to be galloping between the trees. Frisbee-sized windmills "planted" in the ground appeared to have sprung up around the house in place of flowers. Day-Glo rubber balls as tall as the children themselves sat staked to the ground in the central party area. They seemed to have fallen from the sky like big, silly gifts but, in effect, they kept the children from straying too far away. In the middle of it all sat a yellow party table fit for a pint-sized princess and her court. The tablecloth, a massive rubber jigsaw of numbers and letters, looked like a kindergarten lesson animated in blazing Technicolor. A centerpiece of pink gerbera daisies cheerfully smiled out at the children from the fortress of old-fashioned wooden blocks, an easily constructed base built on the geometric lines and simple color scheme of the jigsaw tablemat. Together with the tiny flowers sewn to the edges of each little napkin on the plastic place settings, this fusion of eye-catching colors and playful patterns brought a sparkle to every eye.

The scene was just as merry in and around the schoolhouse. Oversized flower pinwheels in pink and purple stood in for the standard planter, welcoming the children to enter. Inside, the first thing they saw was a chalkboard. But this was no ordinary schoolhouse, and the message on the board was not a homework assignment but a colorful birthday wish from Phoebe's mom and dad. A Crayola-inspired array of colored chalk awaited the children so they could all join in the birthday wishes, and so began an afternoon of bright, visually captivating activities. A cheerful, hand-painted canvas echoing happy wishes for the birthday girl encouraged the kids to create their own little masterpieces when they discovered a circle of easels stocked with paper and finger paints. And if they were looking for a fantastic inspiration, they had only to look up: The ceiling could have floated away for all the jostling, helium-filled polka-dot balloons in candied hues of lavender, pink, yellow, and orange. Never straying from a strict and almost psychedelic color scheme of Play-Doh pink, mango orange, and canary yellow, I created a strange and inviting playroom that extended even the wildest child's dream of the known world. Salvador Dalí, eat your heart out!

# The Alphabet Block Centerpiece

- Place gerbera daisies in simple, square glass vases.

- Glue wooden toy blocks to each other with a hot glue gun to "fence in" each glass vase.

- Place around each vase for a fun centerpiece or runner.

# The Scent

## FRESH AND TOXIN-FREE

I've never actually seen a group of kids stop and smell the roses. Not that they're too preoccupied with their careers, beating the rush-hour crunch, or personal crises. It's just that they don't seem to have an inclination toward the finer fragrances the world has to offer. In fact, from what I can tell most kids seem to be pretty happy sticking their nose in the sandbox or chewing on their own shoes. I have no idea what science has to say on the subject of children and olfactory pleasure, but one thing is certain for you, the party host: It is not important to fuss over a bouquet of lilacs or herb garnishes for a rowdy team of five-year-olds. An obvious point, perhaps, but there's more: *No scent* is a *good scent.*

Think of the familiar parental question, "Do you smell something burning?" Before your party, rid the entire area of anything flammable or toxic. Nix the bottles of OFF! and citronella candles. Opt for water-soluble toxin-free finger paints. Scour the garden for any pesticides or chemical sprays. Finally, lock up any tool shed or garage where paints and wood stains are stored. If you aim for a decidedly fragrance-free party, I promise that none of the children will leave wondering where you got the nerve to skimp on the votive candles; they'll leave safe and secure. You, in turn, will be happy with the knowledge that once all is said and done, you can save the aromatherapy for a soothing bubble bath later on.

# The Touch

## STAINPROOFED AND PROUD

We were not planning on rain but, come to think of it, the party would have continued without a problem. After all, it was designed to endure paint smudges, cupcake icing smears, peanut-butter clumps, juice spills, crushed jellybeans, grilled cheese drippings, and decimated pickles. Why not a little rain? When entertaining for children, focusing on materials is the first and most crucial step (for sanity purposes, anyhow). I always opt for the rubber, plastic, or paper version of whatever I need. A parent's job is half nurture, half wiping up spills, so I figure things should be as simple as possible. Anything gooey or mushy should be able to simply slide off the table with one quick wipe.

This sounds so utterly practical that you might fear for your decor. But don't get in line for that generic drugstore checkered tablecloth just yet! Plastic and rubber can be *très* chic and *très* creative. In fact, once you hit the local Toys R Us you'll discover they figured out the plastic-and-rubber solution long ago. You can make tablecloths out of anything from plastic Twister "boards," to rubber alphabet puzzles (as I have done here), to rubber ducky shower curtains. Most important, while the tots spill to their hearts' content, the parents don't have to take aspirin after aspirin.

## LITTLE BITES FOR LITTLE TYKES

Few parents make the mistake of serving foie gras or poached pears to a table full of tykes with much simpler appetites. But that doesn't answer the question of what kind of dining experience will excite a herd of picky eaters. In my experience, the answer is variety; it is the prospect of a limitless choice between familiar favorites that satisfies these partygoers. With this goal in mind, then, the most important thing to remember when planning a party menu for children is that they don't call them small fries for nothing. Never serve full-sized portions unless you want enormous, half-eaten sandwiches beached like whales on every surface; a bite will do. For Phoebe's party, she and her guests dined on the old standards — finger-sized peanut butter and jelly sandwiches, corn dogs, pizza, grilled cheese, pickles — but the ingredients were fresh and the array of tastes dazzled.

The same principle applied to the dessert course, which drew gasps, sighs, and exclamations when the children found a spread of petite sweets laid out on a pink, polka-dot covered table in the schoolhouse. In place of a birthday cake, they encountered a tray of pink and light blue miniature cupcakes with individual candles, but that was just the beginning. Every face glowed as the children were handed individual plastic trays that held one cupcake in each color, along with brightly colored cotton candy, wedges of candy oranges, delicate sugar-wafer cookies, an ice-cream cone brimming with a rainbow of M&M's, and, finally, a tiny flower-shaped lollipop. Bliss!

# The Sound

## SUNNY DAYS AND SING-ALONGS

Unless your five-year-old guests met at auditions for *The Nutcracker,* the chances for any kind of organized dance sessions are unlikely. In fact, playing vibrant background music for a mass of children can simply result in louder voices, confusion, and mayhem. Having said that, children will almost always sit down and focus on their favorite songs or sing-alongs, if the moment presents itself. I've seen moms hypnotize a herd of distracted kindergarteners with a good round of *Sesame Street* favorites. Come to think of it, you might even start singing along once you hear those familiar lines: "Can you tell me how to get / How to get to Sesame Street? . . ." For Phoebe, we picked a selection of great recognizable songs, from Disney, Sesame Street, and Lesley Gore:

> Lesley Gore: *Sunshine, Lollipops & Rainbows,* "It's My Party!" and "Sunshine, Lollipops, and Rainbows"
>
> *Disney's Greatest Hits,* Vols. 1, 2, and 3
>
> Sesame Street: *Platinum All Time Favorites*
>
> For extra fun, try *Disney's Karaoke Series: Disney's Greatest Hits*

Partying with abandon is hard work. Children and rock stars alike know this, which explains why both tend to be big sleepers. The parents with whom I work, however, often forget. After Phoebe's festivities were over, her mother was full of energy and thus surprised to find Phoebe curled up in bed with a smile on her face. By the time she woke up the next day, the simple clean-up chores had already been done and her mother could only laugh as Phoebe looked around for a sign that yesterday's fun had been more than a fantasy. When her daughter caught sight of the chalkboard full of birthday wishes, she smiled again and fell back into dreams. Like the gift of every lovingly planned birthday party, this one would be reopened in her mind for years and years to come.

HAPPY Birthday

# Tutera Tips

1. Don't forget that adults will be attending the party, too! Have enough grown-up-sized tableware and food for parents to enjoy the fun.

2. When decorating for your child's birthday party, use bright, vivid colors. Children are not only drawn to these colors, they are less likely to leave the areas where they're concentrated.

3. Always check batteries for the camera and/or camcorder the day before the party. If using regular film, remember to order double prints so you can send them to guests afterward. Or, for a sweet thank-you note, take a photo of each guest with the birthday child and mount it on a card with a message.

4. Never pop balloons or let them loose when the festivities are over. They are not biodegradable and are, thus, unsafe for the environment. Instead, have each guest go home with a balloon.

5. Make sure your child's party doesn't go on for too long! Parties for children between the ages of two and five are also bite-sized, normally running from one to two hours.

6. Take the necessary precautions to childproof the party area. If your child's party is by a body of water (pool, ocean, lake, etc.), make sure you have all those areas gated and blocked off. Consider hiring a lifeguard for the party so that you and your guests can feel more relaxed and secure.

7. To thank the parents that helped you, send them home with floral centerpieces.

8. Finger painting is a great activity for a child's party. It keeps kids totally entertained and the final works of art make wonderful, personalized favors for them and their parents. The trick is to provide every little painter with a "dad-sized" T-shirt to protect his or her clothes, and to keep a bucket of water nearby so no one gets caught "red-handed."

9. Have every child write their birthday wishes for the birthday child on a chalkboard. Spray the board with a fixer, available at any hardware store, so the birthday child can always remember the big day.

10. Let siblings invite a special friend over for the day so they won't feel left out. They can either play apart from the party or they can be helpers. To avoid rivalry, give the sibling a special gift as well.

## LOVE GROWS IN THE FOREST: AN ANNIVERSARY PARTY
*for sixteen*

As special occasions go, silver and gold

ANNIVERSARIES CAN BE THE MOST CHALLENGING TO PLAN FOR

ANOTHER PERSON. WHETHER YOU'VE BEEN MARRIED YOURSELF

OR NOT, IF YOU'VE EVER LISTENED TO THE LYRICS OF A GOOD

POP SONG OR SEEN DR. PHIL ON *OPRAH* THEN YOU KNOW SUCH

A MILESTONE IS SERIOUS BUSINESS. HOW DO YOU HONOR A

COMMITMENT THAT IS UTTERLY GRAND, BUT ONLY BECAUSE DAY

AFTER DAY, ONE KISS OR KINDNESS AT A TIME, TWO PEOPLE

HONORED EACH OTHER IN THE SIMPLEST AND PUREST WAY

POSSIBLE — BY TENDING TO THEIR LOVE COME WHATEVER?

*COSMO* DOESN'T HAVE ANY HOW-TO DIAGRAMS FOR *THAT*.

FOR MANY, THE FIRST RESPONSE to this kind of challenge is to rent a fancy banquet hall and let the opulence of the space show the magnitude of the event. And, honestly, I've both planned and attended several truly wonderful anniversaries in such places. But smaller gatherings feel overwhelmed in these immense rooms and some people will never feel at home there anyway. If you really want people to experience the *feeling* of the occasion with the honored lovebirds (and who wouldn't?), scouting a location that captures the unique character of their lives together makes all the difference. As in love itself, the grandest celebrations of love build their wow-factor out of the simplest, most everyday materials.

For Kerry and Leon Carmel, those materials might be a little more rugged than for most. Over the twenty-five wonderful years of marriage they've shared, they've spent most of their time together restoring their historic 1840 home in Connecticut. When their children and friends think of them, they do not think of the Carmels' modern apartment in the city. They think of Kerry, hammer in hand, mounting period-specific sconces on the pine walls; they think of Leon repairing the little quirks that sprung up over the years; they think of Kerry and Leon taking long, winding hikes in the sprawling woods around the house. So, when they asked me to plan their silver anniversary for fourteen guests, I knew that only the great outdoors around their country home would do.

This is the part where I stop rhapsodizing about love and parties and figure out how to make the ten unlandscaped acres around their house feel opulent. Grandeur wasn't a problem: The old, towering trees that lined every clearing on the property served as natural metaphors for the scale of the occasion, the timelessness of Kerry and Leon's love, and their growth together. Once I thought of the dramatic quality of these giants, I knew that a rustic, elegant formal dining arrangement would blend perfectly with the scene. Flowerpots erupting with fresh herbs and orange zinnia would replace the usual vase of cut flowers on a large wood table clothed in a mustard- and rust-colored checked pattern. Mossy urns of rich, green foliage from the property would perch on stone pedestals that blend seamlessly with the forest floor. Dinner plates of the most extravagant onyx would dress up candles and glassware in mustard and amber hues that made the table glow with homey sophistication. Most importantly of all, candles of deep yellow tones, set on iron candelabras and in tiny votives, would guide Kerry, Leon, and their guests through different parts of the twinkling forest to drink and dine as night fell; a journey as romantic and mysterious as love itself.

# The Look

Fusing the rustic with the formal may seem like a troublesome contradiction or a decor disaster waiting to happen. However, it is precisely at the intersection of two seemingly unrelated ideas where I thrive creatively. For one thing, adding a casual, rustic element to a formal party — potted herbs at a sit-down dinner or Spanish moss on antique candelabras — invites guests to *relax into* the formality rather than merely feeling impressed (or oppressed) by it. At the same time, setting a silk-laid table and velvet-upholstered chairs in the middle of a forest nook invites guests to *step up to* the significance and formality of the event rather than feeling like they're attending one more summer yard party.

With this in mind, I set out to create anniversary party decor for the Carmels that was both fabulous and farmhouse, chic and spare. An engraved invitation (created by Christine Traulich at RedBliss Invitations) rimmed with boxwood hedge leaves set the tone when it arrived at guests' homes in an ecru-colored silk box, but that gave only the smallest hint at what was to come. As guests arrived at the actual event, the simple grassy pathway to the cocktail reception was lined — red-carpet style — with bold, yellow sunflower heads. Once there, they found moss-covered wooden tabletops set atop rustic stone pedestals, and small flickering votives illuminating the sunset scene. I chose bright yellow tapered candles, small orange and yellow votive candles, and the odd zinnia blossom to bring a flame of color to the wooded area. But the golden hue of the champagne sparkling in the gloaming offered the finest complement of all to the entire color scheme and, against the texture of the moss and rugged wooden bar surface, reaffirmed the whimsy of field and finery.

The dinner arrangements embroidered on all of these motifs, but at a suitably grand scale. Individual candlesticks from the cocktail party became massive iron candelabras dripping with Spanish moss. The hints at a sun-kissed color palette now blazed brighter with a golden-hued silk-checked tablecloth, bold yellow- and rust-colored napkins, amber glasses, flax-colored place and menu cards, and copper-colored votives, which were dipped in turmeric, paprika, and dried mustard for extra fiery tones. Instead of scattered pots of herbs and leafy greens, a naturally regal centerpiece of plentiful fresh herbs, electric-orange zinnia, moss, ferns, and glossy galax leaves rose from ornate urns beneath the tall, tapered candles with mica shades. For the final touch, pristine silver flatware, brought "down-to-earth" by handles carved into the shape of snapped twigs, were surrounded by plates of pure onyx. Despite all its seeming contradictions, the completed setting, like the couple who inspired it, looked right as rain.

### HOW TO MAKE
# Spice-Rolled Votive Holders

- Paint simple glass votive candleholders with glass paint, making sure to paint in uneven strokes so that he candlelight can shine through.

- Dip the top in regular white glue — about ⅛ inch will do.

- Dip glue-covered edge into dried spices (turmeric, dried mustard, paprika, etc.).

- Allow the spice-covered glue to dry.

- Add a tea light when ready to use.

# The Scent

## HERBAL BOUQUETS

Marriage is like a garden: You've got to weed out the problems, protect it from environmental hazards, and nurture it every day in order to make it last. Kerry and Leon must have learned this early. Their love has been in full bloom for twenty-five years. And, perhaps not by coincidence, the herb garden nestled in a quiet corner of their wooded yard hasn't done so badly either. The moment I caught a glimpse of this virtual forest of bright leafy basil, rosemary, thyme, and mint just outside their kitchen window, I knew what the heart of my "floral" arrangement would be. Instead of the heavy perfume of roses — an old standby of anniversary parties — I limited the flowers in the centerpiece to scent-free zinnia and let the natural fragrance of fresh potted herbs fill the air with invigorating aromas.

This gesture not only made use of the Carmels' many planted herbs, its elemental scents blended beautifully with the simple menu and the rugged scenery around the table. The aromas of vibrant mint and basil carried memories of the loving toasts that were raised earlier, when champagne and fresh herb cocktails were in hand. The *most* significant aspect of this gesture was clear, though: It honored Kerry and Leon's well-spent time together in the garden.

# The Touch

## STONE, MOSS, SILK, AND PEARL

Whenever I find myself in a beautiful natural spot, I'm inclined to just sit down and take it all in. Swept away by the moment, I never seem to think about whether the grass is damp, the sand soggy, or the rocks a little too abrasive for the chinos. We've all returned from a perfect picnic with a grass stain or a sandy shoe, but when entertaining outdoors in high style, the textures of nature must be perceived visually, not underfoot (or tush). For Kerry and Leon's party, I worked with two textures: the rough-hewn to behold and the refined to touch. I covered most surfaces with raw natural textures, like rugged sheet moss, nubby Spanish moss, uneven stone urns, coarse ferns, and leafy zinnia, all of which can be purchased at any garden store. In contrast, the seats, glasses, plates, knives, forks, and napkins — anything, in short, with which the guests would actually come in contact — were all of the smoothest finish. Velvet cushions softened the chairs, while slick onyx plates, amber goblets of fine glass, and pure silk linens added a luxurious touch to the table. In an ideal marriage of nature and nurture, guests experienced delicate comfort even as they perceived the unpolished edges of nature's own striking decor, proving that dining "in the rough" doesn't have to feel that way.

# The Taste

## ENDURING CLASSICS

A twenty-fifth wedding anniversary deserves some real fanfare, but the diverse ages and tastes of the guests at this kind of party also demands a user-friendly menu. And, if you're dining in a natural setting, you'll want to avoid the ungainly presentations and baroque pairings of nouvelle cuisine. That's why the classics work so well for this party: flavors as simple, memorable, and striking as the setting. Of course, as Kerry and Leon know well, the classics can feel fresh and innovative with the right flourishes.

Take, for instance, the herbed champagne cocktails that brought a sprightly but stylish zing to the forest that evening. When I learned that Kerry and Leon were champagne aficionados I asked Thomas Harlander of the Washington, D.C., Park Hyatt to put a spin on the classic *coupe de champagne,* and the results were stellar. A simple leaf of basil or mint floated in each glass of grappa and herb-spiked Moët & Chandon, offering guests the kind of delicacy that awakens the taste buds in high style and, moreover, with a literal taste of their natural surroundings.

The dinner menu itself presented a similar experience of subtly transformed standards, featuring fresh, earthy ingredients. A prawn salad brightened with cucumber, garlic, and lemongrass echoed the sweetness and quiet zip of the champagne, while juicy melon dashed with orange and Grand Marnier added more robust flavors to the mix.

## A Menu to Remember

FIRST COURSE
PRAWN SALAD WITH CUCUMBER, GARLIC, AND LEMONGRASS

SECOND COURSE
MELON WITH ORANGE AND GRAND MARNIER

THIRD COURSE
FILLET OF LAMB WELLINGTON WITH MADEIRA SAUCE

POTATO PUREE WITH GARLIC AND SAGE

PAN-SEARED ASPARAGUS WITH LEMON CITRUS SAUCE

FOURTH COURSE
CHOCOLATE RASPBERRY WINE CAKE

It was these robust, timeless flavors that the rest of the meal built from: a fillet of lamb Wellington with Madeira sauce arrived beside a garlic- and sage-accented puree of potatoes and pan-seared asparagus glazed in lemon. A divine chocolate cake embellished with raspberry and wine capped the evening. The whole feast was glorious enough for the finest occasion, but as timeless as the trees.

## BASIL CHAMPAGNE COCKTAILS

1 cup sugar
1 cup Chardonnay
Handful of basil leaves (about 10)
½ cup grappa
Moët & Chandon champagne

Combine the sugar and Chardonnay in a small saucepan over medium heat and slowly bring it to a boil, stirring continuously until the sugar has dissolved. Add the fresh basil and cook for one half hour on low heat. Stir in grappa and allow the essence to cool overnight. Strain the liquid and pour 1 to 2 tablespoons of the essence into a champagne flute, then top with champagne. Garnish with fresh basil leaf.

# The Sound

## TWO KINDS OF ROMANCE MAKE BEAUTIFUL MUSIC

Unlike the staggered arrivals typical of most dinner parties, Kerry and Leon's guests would be assembled together as they approached the wooded dinner setting. When this rare opportunity presents itself, and all the guests converge on the party in one group filled with anticipation, I love to cue sweeping emotions with a little multimedia fun. In this case, the media was really just a single CD player hidden in the trees, but its effect was monumental. Once guests made their way over the creek to approach the cocktail area they could hear the soaring beauty of Andrea Bocelli's voice lifting up over the trees and beckoning them onward. The seemingly untouched forest suddenly became a virtual opera set, complete with a looming, leafy backdrop that would make the Metropolitan Opera design team swoon. *This* is the power of sound in entertaining: a short nature walk turned into living theater, simultaneously drawing every guest into the enchanting music of Kerry and Leon's epic love story and the space where they'd honor it.

But a peak is a peak; big effects depend on brevity. So, as the cocktail party got under way, I slowly shifted gears from divine romance to earthly romance, and the heart-stopping emotions of Bocelli's music gave way to the more everyday sentiments of love crooned by Dinah Washington and Sonny and Cher. With one simple, if dramatic, sonic gesture, Kerry and Leon's guests would know the connection between those two kinds of romance from now on. Here are some "must-have" musical selections:

Dinah Washington: *Unforgettable,* title song

Shania Twain: *Come on Over,* "You're Still the One"

Israel Kamakawiwo'ole: *Facing Future,* "Over the Rainbow / What a Wonderful World"

Chantal Kreviazuk: *How to Lose a Guy in 10 Days* soundtrack, "Feels Like Home"

Sonny and Cher: *Look at Us,* "I Got You Babe"

Barry White: *The Ultimate Collection,* "You're the First, the Last, My Everything"

Ani DiFranco: "Wishin' and Hopin' " and Diana King, "I Say a Little Prayer" on *My Best Friend's Wedding* soundtrack

*Wicked,* "For Good," featuring the original Broadway cast of *Wicked*

I never like to hear that one of the parties I've planned ended in tears. Then again, when Kerry explained what caused them I understood. Somewhere between the cocktail area and the dinner table, Kerry and Leon's daughter noticed a tree with some carving on it. When she looked more closely, she recognized her parents' initials and the year 1980, when they bought the house. "I'd forgotten all about that tree!" Kerry laughed (and half-sobbed). We can only guess what she and Leon had been doing in the middle of those woods as newlyweds; maybe there is a little *Cosmo* in every lasting marriage. But moments like these are the unexpected gifts of celebrating life in a space where you've also lived it. This time, she assured me, neither she nor her guests would forget carving the year and all of their initials in the very same tree.

# Tutera Tips

1 Nobody likes to dine with mosquitoes and flies, but I'll tell you a secret: Nobody likes dousing their party clothes in OFF!, either. So, when hosting an outdoor dinner party, keep a less-imposing insect repellent, like Skin-So-Soft, on hand as a backup, but spray the party area with any off-the-shelf yard fog one or two days before the event. You and your guests will be glad you did.

2 Send printed anniversary invitations to guests in a silk box lined with decorative elements from the party to come. They won't just create a sense of anticipation and curiosity about the event; they'll serve as mementos to a *very* special occasion. It's also like getting a favor before the party; the box is a perfect place to hold party photos.

3 Leave the cut flowers inside. Potted plants accented with orange or yellow buds make an easy, economical, and appropriate centerpiece for an outdoor dinner table. You can either give the buds as gifts or blend them into your garden when the party's over.

4 Flowers are not just for the table. Line the path with pots of dripping shrubs and blooms for a cheerful "map" to the party.

5 To jazz up plain votive-candle holders with a suitably natural flourish, brush each one with a copper shade of glass paint and dip its rim in dried herbs and spices, like mint, paprika, and turmeric. By the time they dry, you will have unique and fragrant accents for the table!

6 If you have a fresh herb or vegetable garden, why not present a little taste of it as a gift to your guests? Just like mom always said, homemade gifts are the best ones of all.

7 Love is a many-splendored thing. Bring a little of it to the heart of each guest at an anniversary party by writing a different cherished love poem in calligraphy on individual paper fans. Just secure a twig "handle" between two sturdy sheets of paper that match the menus and place cards (the poem should be written on one in advance), then fasten them together with rubber cement. Punch a hole on either side of the twig and then tie a sheer white ribbon around it. Leave one fan on each seat.

8 Don't always rely on nature to produce that "natural" look, especially where moss and leaves are concerned. Use only the store-bought kind on surfaces that your guests will touch, as "the real deal" often holds small (but hungry) bugs.

9　To add to the outdoor look of your dinner, use moss sparingly throughout the table or decorations, reminding your guests that nature is all around them. Accent place cards and planters with it, but also experiment with different shapes. For instance, cover foam spheres in sheet moss to play with the idea of nature and artifice.

10　Take advantage of the Internet! Although you should always have alternate plans to bring an outdoor party in, the extended forecasts available online can help you track how likely that scenario is and plan accordingly.

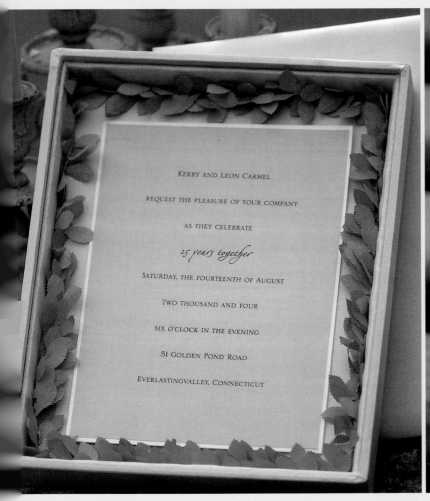

KERRY AND LEON CARMEL

REQUEST THE PLEASURE OF YOUR COMPANY

AS THEY CELEBRATE

*25 years together*

SATURDAY, THE FOURTEENTH OF AUGUST

TWO THOUSAND AND FOUR

SIX O'CLOCK IN THE EVENING

51 GOLDEN POND ROAD

EVERLASTINGVALLEY, CONNECTICUT

# Conclusion

Designing a party that really resonates in someone's imagination is its own reward. In the process of planning and celebrating a special occasion, my clients share their personalities, their dreams, and their happiness with me. In return I try to share mine with them, and that's why I never simply go by the book. Which brings me to the subject of why I wrote *this* book. Creating a one-of-a-kind event—something that really lives up to the name *event*—is never just about some wild eureka moment or a vision of party-planning poetry that beams down from the heavens at night. It's about learning what works and making it your own; it's about introducing the tried, the true, and the traditional into your own life to make it new again (and definitely having a little fun in the process). I always say the party itself is only a percentage of the party plan; you should enjoy every step along the way.

With this end in mind, I've included tips and instructions for how to fashion the details of every party in this book, but I have spent equal time trying to evoke the sensations and the meanings they generate. Likewise, I've tried to introduce the basic steps specific to four unique kinds of parties, from milestone celebrations to cocktail hours, without telling you there's only one way to dance them (a word to the wise, though: avoid the Macarena). So whether you want to re-create one of these events from top to bottom, borrow a few ideas, or simply let a color scheme or combination of flavors and textures wash over you for inspiration, you may be the judge. From my perspective, planning a gathering has all the same charm as attending one: sharing something you value with others. Think of the parties in this book as a kind of creative gift certificate to spend however your imagination wants, keeping in mind that your party should reflect your personality and style.

In the end, however, the "Tutera touch" still depends less on guidelines than on recognizing a personal connection between yourself, your guests, and a totally unique occasion. It's in those little moments when you feel that overwhelming happiness radiating from a guest.

Throughout the course of designing the parties in this book, I had the good fortune to enjoy that feeling on several occasions. For instance, replacing ordinary place cards with old photographs in silver frames for a reunion of lifetime friends, as I did for Jo Ann Atwater's garden dinner, was fun in its own right. But hearing Jo Ann describe the transcendent smiles of her guests as they found their seats? Well, that was something altogether divine. And although I didn't ask Thom and Sally Bowman if the rowboat ride to a formal proposal dinner on a floating dock captured the mischievous streak I saw in them both, the tiny engraving of the boat on the wedding invitation they sent me offered the sweetest answer I could ever want. Above all else, I hope the lessons and ideas in this book help to inspire that same wonderful feeling in you and your guests. Because that's really the amazing thing about giving someone a party that touches their heart through the five senses: it has a way of touching your heart back.

# Acknowledgments

It is through the loving guidance of my parents, Jo Ann and Joe Tutera, that I keep moving forward with my passion. Thank you for giving me the strength and courage to believe that there are endless possibilities. Mom and Dad, thank you for showing me that the core of success begins with love! I thank each member of my family — Pop-Pop, Maria, Nanny, Gregg, Amy, Rich, Mia, Rich, Vergie, and Scott — for always being there.

To my loyal fans, your support and good wishes are a constant motivation. I am excited to share this book with you and hope that it is a new source of inspiration.

There is no such thing as impossible, especially with the help of all these wonderful people who have contributed their time, energy, and resources. My special thanks to Kate Boyle and Executive Chef Gerry Hayden of Amuse Restaurant; Andrew Ginsburg and everyone at DC Rental; Millennium Imports and Belvedere Vodka; Christine Traulich at RedBliss Invitations; Party Cloths; Mondavi Vineyard; Aidan Murphy of Restaurant Associates; Fred Przyborowski of Roof Terrace Restaurant and Bar; Bernadaud China; Unique Table Tops; Suzanne Blizzard of Sonnier & Castle; Pam Marshall and everyone at St. Clements Castle; Michael of Pronto Printers; Anna Weatherly; Sue Kach; Pany Silk Flowers; Allan Munier; and Josephine Lehman of Divine Corporation. Thank you for all your generosity and enthusiasm!

My deepest gratitude to all my special friends and colleagues. Your devotion and enthusiasm have been remarkable throughout the production of this book. A very personal thank-you to Jennifer and Charles Maring, for creating a beautiful cover and for all of the exquisite photographs in this book. You capture a vision of beauty and art through your keen eyes. I look forward to many more creative times together in which we will continue to create unforgettable images.

To Eda Kalkay, my publicist and personal cheerleader. Your enthusiasm and dedication continue to propel me to the next level. Thank you for always being a true and supportive friend.

To my staff, my wonderful artists, who helped make this project fun — special thanks to every one of you at TruMar Media: Ryan Jurica,

Steve Skopick, and Lisa Munier. Thank you all for your assistance, energy, and dedication!

Thank you, Frederica Friedman, my literary agent, for your care, perseverance, and commitment to my vision. Thank you, Kristen Schilo, my literary editor, for your wonderful support and polish. And many thanks to my publisher, Jill Cohen at Bulfinch, for your wisdom, guidance, and erudite vision. I look forward to our partnership ahead. Thank you to each and every one of the Bulfinch Press team who have poured so much of their time and efforts into producing a beautiful book.

A very special thank-you to Ceridwen Morris, whose imagination and creativity are expressed through each word on every page throughout this book. Your dedication to excellence and your talents are a treasured jewel that truly is experienced through all five senses of entertaining. You are an absolute pleasure to work with and I look forward to so many more opportunities ahead.

Most important of all, to Ryan Jurica, my heart and my soul. You make life a constant joy and I look forward to sharing many new chapters of our lives together. Your creative and gifted genius is seen throughout this book, and I thank you from the bottom of my heart. It is love and laughter that have allowed us together to create this exceptional book. I can't imagine celebrating life without you in it. You are my Angel!

Happy entertaining!

# Index